A NAIL
IN A
SURE PLACE

The Importance of "Nails"

by Tim Hansel, Founder
Summit Expedition
Author, *Holy Sweat, You Gotta Keep Dancin'*

I believe that life is meant to be a
daring adventure. In that regard, I have
spent the last eighteen years working
with an incredible wilderness ministry
called Summit Expedition. More than anything else we have hoped to provide
people with an experience that would
remind them that the Christian faith is an
adventure like no other. Nothing surpas-
ses the marvelous privilege of knowing
and serving Jesus Christ.

Fortunately, God never intended for
us to take on this adventure alone. Outside of His own Son, the greatest thing He
has given us is each other.

When I first started rock-climbing,
we used a device called a piton (a small
nail-like object that we pounded into
cracks in the rock) in order to secure ourselves on the more difficult climbs. As the

leader attempted a steep section of the rock, he would "nail" a piton in every ten or fifteen feet, and then link the rope to it with a carabiner, to protect the climbers in case of a fall.

In the same sense, I think that our loving God fastens, or nails, people in our lives for us to hold on to during difficult times. Just as our pitons provided assurance for our fellow climbers, those special people provide us a tangible hope and security when we must face the inevitable challenges and sometimes overwhelming obstacles. Margaret Jensen calls these people "nails in a sure place."

God has gifted this author in a remarkable way. She is an effervescent writer and has an absolutely contagious heart for our Lord. In the following pages, she wants to remind each of us in a powerful way that we can be a "nail in a sure place" for someone else. Jesus told us emphatically that the *primary* way people would know we are His disciples is by the tangible way we love each other.

This book will change your life. I'd like to close by saying boldly to you, "Someone near you is on a difficult climb, and that person needs you."

Christmas 1990
To my dear grandaughter Cheryl. I hope you
enjoy this book as much as I have.
Keep it to read when you are 50!! and again when
you are 60!!! and again when you are as old
as I am, and you will still praise the dear
Lord for the Nail In A Sure Place and others.
Love You dear
Grammy

A NAIL
IN A
SURE PLACE

by
Margaret Jensen

Here's Life Publishers

First printing, June 1989
Second printing, November 1989

Special Hardcover Edition for Family Bookshelf: 1990

Published by
HERE'S LIFE PUBLISHERS, INC.
P. O. Box 1576
San Bernardino, CA 92402

Library of Congress Cataloging-in-Publication Data
Jensen, Margaret T. (Margaret Tweten), 1916-
    A nail in a sure place : holding on when you want to let go /
Margaret Jensen.
        p.   cm.
    ISBN 0-89840-250-6
    1. Christian life—1960-   . 2. Jensen, Margaret T. (Mar-
garet Tweten), 1916-   . I. Title.
BV4501.2.J435   1989
248.4—dc20   89-32074
                        CIP

Unless otherwise indicated, Scripture quotations are from the
King James Version.
Scripture quotations designated NIV are from *The Holy Bible:
New International Version,* © 1973, 1978, 1984 by the Internation-
al Bible Society. Used by permission of Zondervan Bible
Publishers.

Quotes are from Oswald Chambers, *My Utmost for His
Highest,* and C. H. Spurgeon, *The Treasury of David.*

For More Information, Write:

L.I.F.E.—P.O. Box A399, Sydney South 2000, Australia
Campus Crusade for Christ of Canada—Box 300, Vancouver, B.C., V6C 2X3, Canada
Campus Crusade for Christ—Pearl Assurance House, 4 Temple Row, Birmingham, B2 5HG, England
Lay Institute for Evangelism—P.O. Box 8786, Auckland 3, New Zealand
Campus Crusade for Christ—P.O. Box 240, Colombo Court Post Office, Singapore 9117
Great Commission Movement of Nigeria—P.O. Box 500, Jos, Plateau State Nigeria, West Africa
Campus Crusade for Christ International—Arrowhead Springs, San Bernardino, CA 92414, U.S.A.

Dedicated to

Larry Marbry
who used what he had in his hand
for the glory of God
and for my good.

He took a hammer into his hand,
and with it he fastened a nail in a sure place.
From that nail came creative design
and beauty—*my* secure place.

To God be the glory!

CONTENTS

SPECIAL THANKS

In this day of magic computers, I still write on yellow legal
pads—in airports, airplanes, hotel rooms, even
in a car.

When I get back to my beautiful hiding place, I gather all
the notes together. Then the work begins. My husband
Harold takes my penned scrawl and his typewritten pages
fly across the miles. A special thanks to God for you,
Harold, and my thanks for your gift of perseverance and
patience.

Thanks to our son, Ralph, who can take a piece of wood
and create a thing of beauty. He did that for me.
Thanks.

Thanks to Steve Jensen, our nephew, who not only
brought his hammer, but joined his humor to Ralph's. We
had plenty of comedy, some frustration perhaps, but no
tragedy.

Thanks to all the family who keeps urging this grandma to
"go for it."

Thanks to my church family—Myrtle Grove Presbyterian
Church, and our four pastors: Horace Hilton, Jim Glas-
gow, Steve Mattis and Scott Hilborn. These men welcome
me home from my travels and refresh me with their love
and prayers.

Thanks to Les Stobbe, Dan Benson, Jean Bryant, Deena
Anthony, Karla Lenderink, Bob Dykstra, and all the rest
of the staff at Here's Life Publishers, Inc., and to Doris
Fell, for being a special family.

And finally, my thanks to my many friends across the
miles who continue to send messages of their love and
prayers.

INTRODUCTION

"Men return again and again to the few who have mastered the spiritual secret; whose life has been hid with Christ, in God. These are of the old time religion, hung to the nails of the cross."

—Robert Murry McCheyne regarding
Oswald Chambers.

And I will
FASTEN HIM AS A NAIL
IN A SURE PLACE;
and he shall be for a glorious throne
to his father's house.
And they shall hang upon him
all the glory of his father's house.
(Isaiah 22:23,24)

THE
TENT STAKES

The church, with its steeple, had been built by descendants of the farmers who so long ago drove the tent stakes of their faith into the fabric of their community.

Canada Air lifted off the Twin City runway; within moments we were soaring into the Canadian skies, destination: Saskatoon, Saskatchewan.

I peered out of the window and watched the marshmallow clouds tumbling playfully in blue skies. Far below the clouds, earth was playing another game. The prairie looked like a giant chessboard: yellow fields of grain beside squares of black soil; a gigantic fence of towering green spruce etched against the cobalt sky. Farmhouses stood on their squares, refusing to budge, risking a cunning game of chess with 20th century developers and their bulldozers. Red barns and silos formed protective shields, trying to block man's moves against the checkered prairie.

I eased back in my seat and relaxed. I was returning to my "island" — the "place" I had tucked away along the back roads of my mind. My thoughts took flight on the wings of the wind on the prairie — back to sixty years ago when I looked out of a soot-covered window of a train that click, click, clicked over the rails to our new home in Chicago, Illinois. Papa was to be the new pastor of the First Norwegian Baptist Church of Logan Square.

Mama and God had won the battle of the "red linoleum," and with quiet faith she followed Papa into the unknown land. The checkered Canadian prairie, the small house with the cookstove and rocking chair, the outhouse and water wagon belonged to another day. Mama's heart was fixed to obey God. Her feet and her children would follow.

I did not share Mama's strong convictions. In my childish mind I knew that an era was passing and would never return. As the train chugged forward, I kept looking back. The fields of grain, the towering forests reaching to the sky, the galloping hooves of my horse, Dolly, the tractors and plows — and the farmer's son — would be no more. My tears communed with the black cinders.

When we reached Chicago it wasn't long before the banging doors of our second floor flat, playing kick-the-can in back alleys, the clanging of street cars and the roar of elevated trains became the sounds of my new world.

I remembered how, when the July heat baked the bricks of the row houses, I had found a corner on the fire escape and closed my eyes and dreamed of the prairie. Even then I was seeking an "island," a place that could be my haven. It was then that I rode Dolly again over the mud roads from Deacon Salen's farm to Brancepeth. A coyote's lonely call escaped from the woods and I shuddered delightedly—safe on the back of my old faithful. I could feel the wiry mane against my cheek, and I whispered, "Dolly, I love you and I'll remember you forever."

Papa had seen a steeple by faith.
I saw it in reality.

But my joy was short-lived. Mama's call from the steaming kitchen brought me back from my island to be a part of the second floor flat: Mama and Papa and six children. I was twelve, the eldest.

Now, sixty years later in July of 1988, I really was returning to my island. You can go home again. Canada Air had landed me at the Saskatoon airport.

In the terminal a tiny figure came toward me. "Are you Margaret Jensen?" she asked timidly.

"Yes."

"I am Bernice, the one who wrote to you."

I hugged her to me and marveled that this small bird with broken wings could manage to get to the airport. A young woman, her frail body, tiny and fragile had to be cared for by other strong hands. If she fell,

13

someone else had to pick her up. Unable to sit, she had to stand to eat, and then could handle only small amounts of soft food. When she needed transportation she would slide into a car in a prone position.

It was her eyes that drew me, her large blue eyes, windows of a soul that refused to be confined to that frail body. Her spirit soared with the wind and gave the strength of hope to those whose faith was fragile. From her eyes shone the faith of a child and the love of life itself. In her correspondence with me, I had sensed a writing gift of tender beauty. I wondered at the grace of God to fashion this shining nail in her sure place. The Builder knows His tools well.

Later, we drove to Birch Hills, where I was a guest in Norman Thompson's home, the grandson of the original Thompsons where Papa and I had stayed sixty years ago. The water bucket on the well pump and the cookstove of long ago had been replaced with a microwave oven and a dishwasher. But modern conveniences had not changed the surroundings. The land was the same, endless fields against endless skies of blue.

I was here to be the guest speaker at the dedication of the new Lake Park Baptist Church of Birch Hills. Sixty years ago I had stood proudly beside Papa when he drove the tent stakes into the ground. "Ja, ja, Margaret," he said. "Someday, by the grace of God, there will be a church with a steeple reaching to the sky. Ja, you must remember that, Margaret."

I remembered! I stretched my head back. Against the blue skies of Canada the steeple of the new church rose majestically. The church, with its steeple, had been built by descendants of the farmers who so long ago drove the tent stakes of their faith into the fabric of their community. Papa had seen a steeple by faith. I saw it in reality.

Behind the new church the wind blew gently over the yellow fields of grain. Families and friends came from faraway places to join in a mighty anthem of praise:

Summer and winter,
And springtime and harvest . . .
Great is Thy faithfulness,
O God my Father . . .

Music, speakers, pictures from the past, feasting and fellowship blended the days into one great celebration of joy.

"Come outside Margaret, you must see
the Northern Lights.
Look, they're like
dancing horses in the sky."

Finally, when I stood to speak, my heart overflowed with gratitude to God that in my lifetime I should see the harvest from the trees of righteousness that God had planted.

I seemed to see Papa as he pitched the tent, held meetings in schoolhouses, baptized converts in the river, rode dirty roads to bring hope to the despairing and courage to the weak, faith to the fearful and comfort in

15

sorrow. Those farmers, those sturdy, rough-hewn Norwegian men, had cleared the dense forests, plowed the rough fields and kept their covenant with God to seek first His kingdom, and they knew the fields of grain would be added.

They were!

It was on the Thompson farm where I rode the tractor behind Seivert, my first love. Today his lovely daughter was at the piano — grown, mature, smiling. Deacon Salen's farm was where I learned to milk a cow, built my playhouse in the woods and made a stage to tell my stories to the trees. Back then, only the wind applauded.

It was Deacon Salen's daughter Cora who had pumped the organ at the tent meetings. Today she smiled from the audience as we recalled sharing our horse Dolly.

In the crowd of happy faces Bernice, my new friend, my little bird with broken wings, sang a song of joyous faith. The world heard the music and listened.

Tonight I ate my refreshments with the children, the grandchildren of Papa's old friends. They took me by the hand. "Come outside, Margaret, you must see the Northern Lights. Look, they're like dancing horses in the sky, and over here the lights are like rainbows."

The stars were bright against the dark sky. Then slowly the soft lights fell like a curtain drawing their drama to a close.

I remembered reading that "man can tear down

steeples, but cannot remove the stars." God had fastened the stars in a sure place, and I was back in this once familiar place with Papa's same message: "God is the Northern Light who shines into man's darkness."

Just as God had fastened the early farmers as nails in a sure place, their children and grandchildren had tightened the ropes of the faith of their fathers to the same rugged cross that towers o'er the wrecks of time.

We laughed and cried together, but the sound of "Amazing Grace" was carried by the wind, across the ripened fields of grain to the heart of God—and the cloud of witnesses.

Papa's words rang in my ears. "Ja, ja, Margaret, someday there will be a church."

You were right, Papa. Sixty years later the church echoes:

> *When we've been there ten thousand years,*
> *Bright shining as the sun,*
> *We've no less days to sing God's praise*
> *Than when we first begun.*

And:

> *Great is Thy faithfulness,*
> *O God [our] Father . . .*

2

THE HOUSE ON AVENUE J

The small houses with the big lessons seem to have been replaced by big houses and very small lessons.

With the wee hours of early morning came the time to say goodbye to my Canadian prairie and my new friends from Birch Hills. Soon the open road stretched before my host and me as we roared along toward the Saskatoon airport. But I was taking away more than memories. From the great-grandchildren of Birch Hills I carried creative writing, music and art to be placed in my new office in North Carolina. And I had begged for one more favor — to see the house at 510 Avenue J in Saskatoon.

My driver inhaled deeply as we sped along the traffic-free road. "You can smell the fragrance of grain ready for harvest."

I turned to study his sun-bronzed face as he continued talking. "Once you breathe in the smell of ripe barley fields you can never forget the thrill of harvest. No matter how far I travel I can't wait to get home to these fields of waving grain. A man can stand in his own field and as far as the eye can see are the fields of yellow grain with protective fences of tall spruce to break the wind. Against that yellow the fields of flax look like blue lakes."

I smiled inside. I understood his depth of feeling, his love for the land, his satisfaction at harvest time. I was remembering for Papa, and still savoring the rich harvest back at Birch Hills.

I thought of the early settlers who cleared the land by hand, acre by acre. Men held the reins of the horses while guiding the plow to make straight furrows for seed. The sun, rain and winds came, then the harvest. Before the land was cleared the farmers had made a covenant with God to honor the Lord's day to keep it holy. Sunday was kept for church and family; the horses and plows rested.

Three generations later, the tractors are silent on the Lord's day. Church and family fill the day of rest. In their own way, the fourth generation remembers. One by one, the members of the athletic team decided that Sunday was special and they would not attend the practice session. The coach changed the practice day.

Faith of our fathers, Living still.

Papa never thought he did anything that great — just cleared the roots of unbelief from the hearts of men and plowed in the promises of God. The winds of adversity, the sunshine of joy, the rains of sorrow swept over the fields of humanity. Through it all the faithfulness of a loving heavenly Father, the God of grace, love and mercy, gathered a harvest called the church. Out of the "all things" God works for good.

We arrived at Saskatoon at 5:30 A.M. My driver arched his brows as he glanced at his watch. "Well, Margaret," he smiled, "there's just enough time to see the house on Avenue J."

That one-fourth bar of soap had led to a multiplied feast–and an answered prayer for a barren "Hannah."

There it was! It looked so small, like a one-car garage. Yet in my heart I saw a home, bigger than life, with Mama's cookstove and rocking chair in it. In the corner I visualized the water tank—and the horses pulling the water wagon (25¢ a tank). The outhouse with Mama's starched curtains had stood at the end of the path. Mama was convinced the unpardonable sin was dirt, and the curtains were necessary!

I could almost hear the squeak of the rocker, and I marveled at how five children had lived there, and found ample room in Mama's lap. From that rocker we learned our theology, big lessons of faith in a tiny house.

My memory camera kept clicking while tears filled my eyes. Other small houses now surrounded the house on Avenue J but everything was quiet—the world was still asleep at 5:30 A.M.—and I heard the sounds of yesterday.

21

Mama was always there: baking, scrubbing, stirring her famous soup, washing clothes, and ironing with the irons heated on the stove, while the smell of Linet Starch filled the kitchen.

Mama's starched apron crackled. When she held us she smelled of Palmolive soap and Raleigh's shampoo. Godliness and cleanliness went together.

I remembered the time she ran out of soap, a calamity in a Norwegian household. We all walked to childless Mrs. Johannesen's house. "Could you spare a little soap?" Mama asked. "I need to wash clothes."

"Oh, ja, I have a half-bar of Fels Naptha and I will cut it in half for you, Mrs. Tweten."

"Do you have food?" Mama asked.

"No," Mrs. Johannesen answered hesitantly, "but I have a bag of bones."

"Oh, ja. Vell, I have some vegetables," Mama told her. "I'll take the bones and cook soup, and you come for supper. I have baked bread so there is plenty." We turned and walked home with the bag of bones and our small piece of soap.

In the quiet of the early morning now I could hear again the joy of laughter around that kitchen table and the soup and homemade bread added to the blessings of a settled faith.

"Give and it shall be given," Papa had preached from the pulpit. That one-fourth bar of soap had led to a multiplied feast — as well as an answered prayer for a barren Hannah. Mama and Mrs Johannesen knelt in prayer that day and another day came when a child was born to Mrs. Johannesen.

My mental camera kept clicking while I played a rerun of dipping sugar lumps in Mama's coffee, trimming the Christmas tree with paper ornaments, building skating rinks and toboggan slides in the back yard.

The big lessons of faith are changeless in our changing world.

While Papa traveled the country roads, Mama taught the lessons of faith from everyday living. In the distance I saw where we had picked violets in the spring, and I felt choked and tearful as I remembered.

It was in this small house that my stories were born – The High Button Shoes, The Missionary Barrel, The Bowl of Cherries, The Saturday Night Bath, and many, many other valuable lessons of faith.

My host touched my arm and reminded me that it was time to go. "I had forgotten how small the house was," I told him as we went back to the car. "I only remembered the big lessons. Mama was bigger than life, a nail fastened in a sure place. I'll never forget that tiny house."

His smile seemed to say, "Like my fields of grain."

My heart ached for children who come home to spacious rooms filled with loneliness. Our culture has yanked out so many of the nails that hold the fabric of our society together. We Twetens had been poor – but we had been rich.

23

My gracious host nudged me to the airport where I would say goodbye to new friends gathered there.

I heard the words again, "It is almost harvest time," and I can breathe in the fragrance of waving grain. Somehow in my heart I heard, "It's harvest time, Margaret. God is getting ready to harvest the fields where the wheat and tares of humanity have grown together."

My heart answered, "Lord, keep me true, for there are those who trust me. I will just keep telling the old, old story of Jesus and His love."

It was time to go home to the warm ocean breezes blowing through the pampas grass of North Carolina. The small houses with the big lessons seem to have been replaced by big houses and very small lessons. I longed to share the message with the beautiful young mothers: Perhaps we need to check our faith foundation and rebuild. The beloved people in the houses of today need to know, need to sing:

> *On Christ, the solid Rock, I stand;*
> *All other ground is sinking sand* . . .

"Please fasten your seat belts," announced the flight attendant. "We will be landing in Wilmington, North Carolina."

I was happy to be home again, home with Harold and the family. Always, however, there would be the wind on the prairie, and the tiny house on Avenue J would remind me that the big lessons of faith are changeless in our changing world. Harold would understand when I told him.

24

THE GRANDFATHER CLOCK

. . . a reminder of the good times,
the hard times, the times of joy
and the times of sorrow,
but also that the faithful Father
always kept your times in His hand."

The clock stopped! Our 50th anniversary clock.

The melodious chimes were silent and I missed the rhythmic ticktock that brought us companionship and comfort in a quiet house.

When the clock man came, I poured out my story, recalling the memory of the gift of love from our children—the magnificent clock that now was silent.

"No problem," his actions seemed to say. "I'll get it ticking again."

How often Harold and I had looked at the clocks

in the "Clock House" at the Cotton Exchange in Wilmington. But we never dared to dream of the reality of owning one. And here was the expert. With a minor adjustment he brought the sound of chimes back into the quiet house. Then he was gone, back to his house of clocks, but the memory of the gift had been stirred up.

It was our 50th wedding anniversary.

Our granddaughters, seven-year-old Kathryn and ten-year-old Sarah, seemed to think the entire event was planned for them. "We want long dresses, Grammy," one of them said.

"So we can 'swish' down the aisle," the other added.

They had their wish. Long white eyelet dresses, with crinoline slips and satin bows made "swishing" a delight. They carried balloons lettered with "I love Papa, and I love Grandma," and escorted Harold and me into the fellowship hall of Myrtle Grove Presbyterian Church. Family and friends had gathered from far and near to join in our joyous celebration.

Our daughter Janice and daughter-in-law Chris had kept their plans a secret. Now we saw it all. Tables, flowers, and decorations done in soft blue and peach colors. At the entrance stood a mannequin dressed in my wedding gown, with old-fashioned shoes and veil. Harold, tall and stately, instinctively reached over to kiss the motionless bride.

Beside the bride stood a small table that had been a wedding gift from Tom and Gladys, long-ago friends. The table had been painted through the years in Joseph's coat of many colors. But Ralph, our son, had refinished it to its original walnut beauty so it stood beside the mannequin bride with new dignity.

Friends of long standing gathered with the new friends and with the original wedding party and their families. Howard Jensen, Harold's brother and best man, introduced the wedding party.

Jeanelle, my youngest sister, was the flower girl who dropped one petal at a time — slowly, very slowly walking the long aisle, oblivious to anything except the petals she carefully selected.

When the wedding picture was being taken, she floored the photographer with, "I think I'm getting sick."

We all called out, "Smile first!" She did.

Joyce was the junior bridesmaid who could sing like an angel and jitterbug with the best of them. Papa only heard the song. Howard recalled falling in love with Joyce, that cute little blonde, and how he had returned from the war and married her.

"She's still a cute blonde," he added.

Doris, my bridesmaid, was the one who managed to go to Wheaton College with $100.00 and a dream. Grace, my maid of honor, always managed to do the right thing at the right time and through the years had kept the family ties strong.

Stories and songs filled the evening of feasting and fellowship. Together we sang, "God leads His dear children along."

Then Joyce sang, "He giveth more grace when the burdens grow greater." The years seemed to roll back to the special days of grace. Through it all we learned to trust Him.

Harold and I shared—admitting aloud—that fifty years of marriage also had its difficult times. "But the nail in a sure place was our covenant with God and with each other. The nail held!" we told them.

"Someday I will make white nightgowns for my girls with new material, with embroidered bluebirds."

Our memory books of that evening are filled with cards, pictures, and special greetings from family and friends from around the entire world. There was also the gift of a future trip to Norway. Janice and her husband Jud Carlberg and Ralph and Chris had brought the past and present together, and even included a glimpse into the future, all in a joyful celebration with family and friends.

"You will see on the table," Janice announced, "the bluebirds in the decorative wreaths.

"The tiny bluebirds are a reminder of my grandmother, Bestemör (grandmother in Norwegian) when she said, 'Someday I will make white nightgowns for my girls with new material, with embroidered bluebirds.' "

Janice continued the story:

"New material, Mama?" the girls asked.

"Ja, new material — someday."

"When, Mama?"

"Ja, I don't know ven — I yust know I vill!"

The winters were long, and the snow piled high. Year after year the winter winds blew around the small house. "But do you know what comes next?" Mama would ask. "Spring! The next thing to come is spring, and then come the bluebirds — bluebirds of promise and happiness."

But it seemed that the white nightgowns never came.

The days and months turned into years, and finally the day did come. There in lovely wrapped boxes were the white nightgowns with the little embroidered bluebirds. Bestemör's promise had come true.

"Remember, children," Mama said smiling, "when winter comes, the next thing to come is spring."

As Jan recited the story of the nightgowns, she seemed so much like Mama — the Tweten lilt in her voice, the confident smile.

"When the winter of the soul comes, even then, the next thing to come is spring — God's promises never fail," Jan concluded. "We cry out in the winter of the soul, 'When, Lord?' and God answers, 'You don't know when, but I do.' "

* * *

Then the clock!

When Jan presented that gift of love she said,

"Mom and Dad, this clock is a reminder of the good times, the hard times, the times of joy and the times of sorrow, but also that the faithful Father always kept your times in His hand."

The clock repairman is gone now. His truck is out of sight. He couldn't know the memories he brought back of the day our children gave the gift of the grandfather clock to us.

"And how do you think?" said the old father clock,
"That I feel toward this multiplied flock?
   I feel like using my hands in applause
   For the way they support the homemaker's cause.
   They show by the joy there is in life
   That home is a pleasure, not misery and strife.
   And when they say grace at the family board,
   I almost stop ticking to worship the Lord."[1]

* * *

P.S. Now I know why the Jensen clock stopped!

---

1   Barton Rees Poque, "Old Father Clock," *Ideals* (May 1964), 21:3, p. 22. Used by permission.

TAKE WITH YOU WORDS

"So what's so different between us and the Christians coming out of your churches? Who needs changing?"

T he writer's conference was over. Across the lecture hall I heard the sound of shuffling papers, snapping briefcases, quick goodbyes and the echoes of many retreating footsteps.

But Chuck Colson's words lingered in the room. "We are writers who are Christians," he had said. "We need to send the written message into the culture of our day, a culture increasingly hostile to the Christian message."

Somewhere in the background of my mind, I'd had a vision of eager hands, outstretched to receive the message: "For God so loved the world . . ."

With Chuck Colson's words came reality. Instead of outstretched hands, I now seemed to see an indifferent shrug of shoulders and I heard a cynical, "So what?"

I had a mental picture of myself calling out defensively, " 'So what'?! Don't you know that this Jesus, this Son of God, can change your life?"

The cross of dark, stark wood spoke of God's love stretched out to the millions who pass by. And to me.

With a deep sadness I could almost hear their answer: "So what's so different between us and the Christians coming out of your churches? Who needs changing?"

I left the lecture hall and moved with the crowd of conference campers. I turned in my dorm key and picked up my luggage to return to Wilmington.

My thoughts soared with the plane. Mental notes of all that I had heard seemed to gather in unruly fashion, billowing with the clouds. "Take with you words, and turn men's hearts toward God," resounded in my heart.

Across the blurred memory of faces and words, I retraced my quiet journey through the Billy Graham Museum at Wheaton College. I recalled passing the lifelike figures of men of God who, with words, had changed nations for God.

There were living sounds of Billy Graham's words

of life reaching into the far continents of earth. Letters hung in the museum — words that carried the hopes and fears of all the years, mail, from all over. Wonderful words of life — words like shining nails in a sure place.

I found myself mentally walking alone through the dark carpeted night toward the cross — *"the old rugged cross so despised by the world,"* the cross that towers o'er the wrecks of time. I bowed in humble thanksgiving. I didn't want to leave, the image was so real. It was quiet and that cross of dark, stark wood spoke of God's love stretched out to the millions who pass by. And to me.

In my mind my feet moved slowly back into the widening expanse of blue skies and billowing white clouds, like the dawning of a new earth. The music of Alleluias in my heart rang out the glorious resurrection message:

> *The cross is empty!*
> *The tomb is empty!*
> *He is alive!*
> *He is coming again!*

The great evangelists of the past and present stand like giants, ever pointing to the cross. But somehow, in that sacred place, they all seemed to kneel in humble adoration. The message they proclaimed was eternal.

"Take with you words," I heard once more. Words like nails in a sure place, men like giant nails in a sure place. The cross — God's nail in a sure place.

I opened my journal and read, "The shadow of the cross fell across the world. Night swallowed the sky.

Rocks hurtled off mountains. Tombs ripped open. The veil in the temple was rent."[1]

When the Son of God was dying, every corner of the earth felt the agony, from the mountains to the temple veil. What had been closed was now open.

Now my heart rolled with the majestic billowing clouds outside my plane window. The expanse of sky called out, "He is alive!"

I looked around at my fellow travelers—some of them asleep, others sipping wine or reading papers. While I heard the music of the ages in my soul, the world around me slumbered. Yet I sat safe, secure in the shadow of the cross. "Jesus," I whispered, "I'm sorry the world isn't listening, but I want to say thank You."

1   Oswald Chambers, *My Utmost for His Highest*.

5

IRON STANCHIONS

Begin where you are–you are God's nail in a sure place.

During a recent mountain retreat, I stood before my audience and told them a story I had heard a few years before.

Majestic cliffs rose high above a rocky seacoast. The currents below swept passing fishing boats into the dangerous inlet causing them to crash against the rocks.

One day a certain young fisherman came too close to the dangerous cove and his fishing boat was dashed against the rocks. The fisherman, an expert swimmer, noticed a ledge of safety, high above the rocky coast. He knew he could make it! He swam with all of his might and reached the cliff. But, sadly, tide and time had washed it as smooth as glass. There was nothing to hold on to. The man was washed back out to sea. The ledge of safety was beyond his reach.

An old minister heard about the fisherman and, determined to save the lives of others like him, he chiseled steps into the slippery cliff. Then the old man died and once again tide and time washed the cliff as smooth as glass.

When a young minister heard the story, he also became concerned about the lives of the fishermen, so he drove iron stanchions into the cliff, and attached a rope, running from each stanchion to the next, and fastened to each as it went. That rope would help a victim reach the place of safety.

I looked over my audience of beautiful women and I knew they each would be returning to their own "slippery cliffs." They would need something to hold to. I said, "Today, I want to drive some iron stanchions into this slippery cliff called life.

"Eternal truths never change; they are the iron stanchions for us to hold on to while God fastens us as nails in a sure place. You might be the only nail in your family, or business, or community, just one lone nail, but God will provide a way for you to *hang in there*.

"In the book of Jeremiah, I read of the pleadings of a sovereign God with a rebellious nation. 'How can you exchange the one true God, the God who led you through the Red Sea, who fed you manna and gave you water, how can you exchange this living God for gods of silver and gold?' "

36

I went on to tell the women that our culture around us is offering lesser gods as the one true God. Yet eternal truth never changes.

We often feel loose, or rusty, or even crooked; but we can hang in there when we hold to this **first** strong iron stanchion: *"In the beginning God"; and for all eternity, God.*

A communist philosopher once said that it was America's faith in a transcendent God that gave the dynamo to her society. The world wants a secular equivalent. There is none!

God's Word is full of the promises,
but then comes the battle
to believe those promises.

We must give our children reasons to believe, for doubt blows like a gentle breeze across the minds of our youth. We must know what we believe to be that nail in a sure place. I told the women, "When we know that God is in the beginning, and at the end, then we also know He has a plan for the in-between. Jesus is the Way!"

No one can know the God of the beginning and the end, except through a childlike faith in God's Son, Jesus Christ. The greatest power in our lives is the atonement, the at-one-ment with God: His redemptive work, His cleansing blood, His forgiveness, and His power. What we believe about the atonement will affect every aspect of our lives.

Oswald Chambers says, "The Holy Spirit is deity

37

in proceeding power, who applies the atonement to our experience, and works in us the nature of Jesus."

Blessed assurance, Jesus is mine!

The **second** iron stanchion is *the Word of God, the Bible.*

> For ever, O LORD, thy word is settled in heaven (Psalm 119:89).

Translations come and go, but the truth of the living Word remains. Doctrinal views may differ, but the great Truth, Jesus Christ the Son of the living God, never changes.

> For God so loved the world, that he gave his only begotten Son, that whosoever believeth in him should not perish, but have everlasting life (John 3:16).

> These things [are] *written* that ye may believe" (1 John 5:13).

> The Word of God is quick, and powerful (Hebrews 4:12).

The **third** iron stanchion relates to *the promises of God.*

> Lo, I am with you" (Matthew 28:20).

> I will never leave thee" (Hebrews 13:5).

> Fear not; I will send [the Comforter] unto you . . . he will guide you into all truth" (John 16:7,13).

God's Word is full of the promises, but then comes the battle to believe those promises. The battle is won in the secret place of the will and we must make a definite act of the will to *accept* God's redemptive plan through faith, **believe** the Word of God, and **receive** the promises of God. The test is **obedience** to the third stanchion.

The grace of God, plus our obedience, will make us those exceptional nails in tough places. God's redemptive power moves on the track of obedience.

Trust and obey,
for there's no other way . . .

We usually know what to do, but we would rather substitute Bible study or dedicated service for obedience.

God says *obedience* comes first.

When God's redemption comes to a point of obedience in a human soul, it always creates. "Create in me a clean heart, O God" (Psalm 51:18) follows obedience.

I always enjoy craft fairs. I watch in wonder when people gravitate toward a simpler time—the country look, the old spinning wheel, rag dolls and quilts. It seems we want to return, in memory, to our roots.

Some people have roots they never want to return to—painful memories and unbelievable heartbreaks. More than once, I've heard someone say, "Where do I begin? I never had a family like yours, Margaret. No one taught me about faith in God."

My answer is always the same, "Begin where you are."

"But I have no roots!" the person will protest.

"You do now," I insist, "for you are rooted in

39

Christ, and you can go back to your roots, to the very heart of God."

Someday God will wipe the tears from the eyes of those wounded by painful memories. But in the meantime, He can give His unspeakable peace, His love, His joy.

Hold on to these iron stanchions! Receive God's so great salvation. Believe His everlasting Word. Obey Him. The promises are for each one of us.

Begin where you are—you are God's nail in a sure place.

On Christ the solid Rock I stand;
All other ground is sinking sand.

6

MY DAY IN COURT

*Someday, we will all stand before
the Judge of all the earth. By God's grace
we will hear, "Not guilty!"*

C had, our number one grandson, maneuvered his surfboard into the back and a portion of the front seat of my car. Together we eased out of the driveway.

"Thanks, Grammy," he muttered between bites of whatever he had grabbed to eat.

With out-of-town relatives, cousins and grandchildren, our cars kept a shuttle service going from our house to Wrightsville Beach.

"The waves are just right this time of the morning," Chad told me between swallows.

We chatted about the great time we had at our

50th wedding anniversary party. Now each generation made separate plans—most of the time that meant the ocean. I kept my hands steady on the wheel, down Wrightsville Avenue at an even 55 miles an hour. Then I slowed to 45. We kept laughing and talking, mostly about surfing. Suddenly, out of nowhere, a blue light began flashing behind me.

I braked to a stop on the side of the road and a young officer wanted to see my picture. At that hour of the morning I didn't look much like my picture—and it wasn't even my best side. He looked at the surfboard, then at me, his brows arched.

I had entered the never-never-land of Wrightsville Beach, just over the bridge where the sign reads 35 m.p.h.!

"But I never had a ticket before," I protested, "not even a parking ticket! Couldn't you just give me a warning?" Now I was wailing.

The young officer kept writing—I was making his day! I cried tears of humiliation and frustration, and Chad slipped lower behind the surfboard and then remained motionless.

I tried to explain that we had been talking and were over the bridge before I knew it, but the policeman kept writing.

"Perhaps the judge will show mercy," he said as he handed me the summons.

By the time we got to the beach, Chad's waves weren't that great and my fun had rolled out with the tide. *I knew I'd have to face Harold!*

42

He did not take to it lightly. "Oh, no! You didn't! That's where tourists get caught, not someone who knows that bridge and 35 m.p.h. like the back of your hand."

I didn't protest. Harold and I had weathered fifty years together. We'd make it through my first speeding ticket.

"Grandma got a ticket for speeding!" Chad announced, and the word spread!

"How do you plead?" he asked. Never had I felt so guilty!

"It's just not fair," I moaned. And, "No, I won't just *bite the bullet.*" And finally, "I am going to court!"

"Grandma is going to court!" the grandchildren repeated. They loved it!

And so it came to pass that at 9 A.M. one morning I walked up the courthouse steps and into the courtroom along with other lawbreakers of New Hanover County. Some shuffled in, others took it in stride. Some looked as though they were in familiar territory. One young man eased in beside me. "This is my first time," he admitted.

"Mine, too." We became instant friends—both terrified!

Lawyers, clerks and police personnel seemed to swarm around the place like bees. Guilt engulfed me. I was ready to plead guilty to anything.

The door opened, we were called to order and we

were instructed to "all stand" as the "Honorable Judge
_____" came to the bench. The gavel sounded and
court was in session. I glanced around at the two
hundred or so people around me; they all seemed so
young. I felt like a terrified Grandma Moses about to
be executed.

Then my name was called: "Margaret Jensen."

As I proceeded to the bench, I acutely felt every
eye on me. I stood before the judge, trembling.

"How do you plead?" he asked.

"Guilty, your honor." Never had I felt so guilty.

The clerk smiled and turned to the judge, "Your
honor, she is a writer, and has spoken in our church."

Oh, no, I moaned inwardly. *Someone knows me.*

The judge looked serious, but his eyes twinkled.
"What explanation do you have, Mrs. Jensen?"

For writing? I wondered. *Or for speeding?*

I told him about the anniversary celebration and
about all the relatives in town. I mumbled about the
surf and needing to get Chad to the beach in time to
catch the good waves.

"Fifty years to the same man?" someone asked.

"No, I changed him."

Now the judge was smiling. "Congratulations!"

"Thank you," I managed.

"Now, what kind of books do you write?" he asked,
his eyes still amused.

44

"That good things can happen out of bad situations."

"Perhaps something good will come out of this situation," he suggested.

"I'm counting on it, your honor."

Then in a deep, professional tone he said, "Fine, forty dollars. Case dismissed." The gavel sound was sharp. "Next case."

I paid the fine and went home. Later, I wrote in my journal: *Someday, we will all stand before the Judge of the whole earth. By God's grace we will hear, "Not guilty."*

* * *

The next day I packed my bags to speak at a Canadian youth conference. When I returned home I had an invitation from "my" judge to attend Juvenile Court and listen to the heartbreak of a crying world.

I watched the compassionate judge attempt to solve problems he never created. Social workers and young lawyers worked together to salvage the abused bodies and souls from the wreckage of a fragmented society.

I read somewhere that it takes one million laws to implement the Ten Commandments. But what happens when God's standards, nails in a sure place, are torn from the fabric of our society? Can man's changing rules repair the unraveling of that fabric? God's standards are changeless; man's rules change with the times. But these young people in Juvenile Court, some

45

of them with serious offenses, could well be ignorant of God and the Ten Commandments.

As I watched them, I kept thinking that when man is accountable to no one, there is no accounting for what man can do. In the beginning of our great nation, the home, school, and church had closed ranks to teach our children that we are accountable to God. The moral and spiritual fiber was the strong thread of our culture; and laws based on the law of Moses, God's standards, had made America a special nation, under God, with liberty and justice for all, even for those who do not believe in God.

> *When man is accountable to no one, there is no accounting for what man can do.*

Forty years ago our school children stood before the authoritative figure, the teacher, to plead guilty to chewing gum in class, throwing spitballs, coming in tardy, not emptying the wastebaskets, or failing to clean the blackboards properly.

Today, a generation later, school children come to a courtroom and stand before a judge. Now they are charged with theft, assault, vandalism, rape and murder. Teenage pregnancy, abortion, drugs and liquor comprise a rebellion against authority that emerges as a subculture of its own. I sat there knowing that when God was dethroned in our classrooms, the children's accountability was reduced because it was turned from the highest power and toward peer pressure.

I could not—would not—accept that these juve-

46

niles were totally hopeless, or that they had no place in today's society. I knew they had not been forgotten in God's redemptive plan.

I love children and young people. I had grown up in a home that was neither rich nor fancy. Often we were uprooted when Papa was called to a new ministry, but my siblings and I had known love. We had not escaped strict discipline. We were pointed early toward the straight and narrow, but each also made the choice to walk that way.

Many of these young people had not known a loving Mama and Papa. Some of them had. But had they heard about Jesus? Did they know about the straight and narrow? In our fragmented society, had they even heard that God loves them? They had the right to at least make the choice. I was confident that there must be a way to mend the unraveled fabric of society. There is!

In the beginning, *God!*

To know Him, that He exists, is the one iron stanchion in this slippery cliff called life.

I've reflected often since my day in Juvenile Court that across the pages of history they had come—the men and women who believed God. Men like St. Augustine, John Calvin, Martin Luther, John Knox, and many others, had stood like giants to ax the error of their society. Today men ax the truth.

When men ax the trees in the rain forests of South America and make their own rules, the balance of nature is disrupted. When men ax God's truth, the bal-

47

ance of all society is disrupted. But there's always some-one calling for truth.

Chuck Colson, in *Kingdoms in Conflict*,[1] tells us that during the Industrial Revolution in England the clear sounding voice of Charles Wesley called to the masses, "Jesus is the way, the truth and the life." Social change came when the heart of man was changed, and with it, for one thing, children came out of the workhouses.

Man's laws made slaves. God's laws set men free. In England in the 1700s a statesman, William Wilberforce, cried out against slavery. For a time his voice was drowned by the cry for silver and gold, but after a decade the voices of godly men were heard. William Wilberforce had won! God's law was changeless. In 1807 slave trade was abolished.

An English Lord cried out against abolitionists, "Things have come to a pretty pass when religion is allowed to invade public life."

Certainly the men and women torn from their homes and layered in ships to be sold to the highest bidder would not agree — but no one asked them.

Across the ocean in the young America, a craggy-faced woodcutter came down life's road; his tall, gaunt frame filled the White House. Abraham Lincoln's message of freedom filled the world.

God's law prevailed.

---

1   Charles Colson, Kingdoms in Conflict (Grand Rapids: Zondervan, 1987).

Someone had to speak for those who cannot speak for themselves.

Someone did.

General Booth spoke for the homeless and poor, and a door of hope, the Salvation Army, was opened. God's love invaded the public arena.

Across the jungles and deserts of Africa, David Livingstone carved a path to reach the souls of men. "Greater love hath no man than this, that a man lay down his life for his friends" (John 15:13). David Livingstone's heart of love is buried in Africa while his body is buried in Westminster Abbey.

---

*My faith mounts,
for rising up out of our manmade laws,
young men and women still come,
and they dare to invade
the secular arena with their deep
faith in God.*

Out of an "enlightened" age, which has held unsurpassed exploits in science and technology, a hysterical voice screamed new laws into existence in the 20th century — laws that determined who should be the master race and who should go to gas ovens. A gentle clockmaker from Holland dared to enter that arena with his deep faith in God's law. Only Corrie Ten Boom, one of his daughters, survived the death camps. Her message to the the world was that everyone should remember: There is no pit so deep that God's love cannot reach those at the very bottom.

I read this statement somewhere, and it made a profound impression on me: "The soul has to find and hold its ground against hostile forces, sometimes embodied in ideas which deny its very existence."

What about today? Will the soul of America speak for the young whose minds have been battered by man-made rules that defy the law of God? And who will speak for the unborn generations?

I hear in my heart the clanging of an iron gate and remember what I saw. Now a gentle grandmother sits behind prison walls. She spoke for one whose right to live was denied by man's law.

Like mountain streams they still come: the builders and teachers. They come with Bibles and stethoscopes, hammers and saws, blackboards and chalk. They come with shovels and hoes, pen and paper, like refreshing streams of living water to a scorched earth.

They build churches and schools, hospitals and homes, in the faraway places of jungles and deserts. Lonely graves mark the places where some of them gave their all.

Rising out of the slums and the workhouses, the jungles and the deserts, the city ghettos, the concentration camps and the prisons, they come, those who have heard: "In the beginning, God . . ."; and, "God so loved" them.

My faith mounts, for rising up out of our man-made laws, young men and women still come, and they dare to invade the secular arena with their deep faith in God. They go to prisons, inner cities, near and faraway places, to the lonely and homeless who have lost their way.

They come from around the world: the East and the West, North and South. They come through cultural diversities with the same message: "In the beginning, God . . . " This God we serve has a plan for the youth of the world, and because of this, love has walked into the marketplace.

One day the gavel will sound. High Court will be ended. The Judge of all the earth will say, "Well done, good and faithful servants."

God remembers when the world forgets. Someone speaks for those who cannot speak for themselves.

* * *

P.S. Dear Lord, help me to remember my day in court. Help us all to turn off the dissonant music of our culture and to pray that our ears will hear Your still small voice saying, "This is the way; walk ye in it."

7

MARRIAGE AND HOUSE UNDER CONSTRUCTION

Chad said it all. "Grammy's house small? No way! There's always room for us." The same house, the same street, the same yard . . . Love just stretched the walls.

It began in the fall of 1987.

Janice (our daughter) pounded a sign into the ground in the front yard of our house in Wilmington. The letters were bold, the message clear:

> MARRIAGE AND HOUSE
> UNDER CONSTRUCTION

The porch and carport walls had been torn down. Debris multiplied until the back yard looked like *Sanford and Son*. The back steps consisted of cement blocks perched precariously on makeshift slabs. Our once cozy home looked like a bombed out war zone. The only thing settled was the dust.

Larry Marbry, a young builder, had taken one look at my dining and kitchen tables piled with yellow pads and mail. He shook his head. "You need a room for writing!" he said.

Believe me, that was the understatement of the year.

I wrote in the kitchen. Harold typed in the dining room, which was also part of the living room. At the end of each day I cleared the tables, and the boxes went under the bed. I let the long side of the bedspread hang down on the side where the boxes were so they wouldn't show.

When the family came to visit, cots emerged from the utility building and lined the living room like a camp dormitory.

Larry was determined to do something about the mess. "I'm going to draw up plans to give you some room — and a special writing room. Margaret, if you and Harold will buy the material, I'll do the building. We'll pay as we go and we'll look for bargains. This is my gift back to God, and my gift of love to you."

He grinned. "I can't sing like my wife Reneé or tell stories or preach, but I can build! Whatever is in our hand — that is what we give back to God."

And it came to pass. The plans were drawn and Larry took a hammer into his hand, and the nails found a sure place.

Harold reluctantly cut down our productive pear tree. We all remembered how we canned pears during hurricane Diane. Pears blew everywhere. That was the time for pears. Now is the time for writing. For everything, there is a season. Instead of pear blossoms, there bloomed a beautiful two car garage with an office room across the back for writing.

This definitely was the day the Lord had made, and no one had better get in the way.
Even trembling traffic lights turned green when we approached.

Machinery filled the garage so the cars stayed outside. The sounds of saws and hammers blended with the laughter and jokes. My camera caught pictures of Larry's eighty-seven-year-old grandfather on a ladder, setting the pace for the young. Harold kept supplies coming while Ralph, Steve and the boys, Shawn and Eric, reviewed basketball scores and pounded nails.

Perfectionist Larry checked, measured and rechecked plans and workmanship until phase one was completed. I could move my papers and boxes into the new office. I had a place to write!

Inside the house, sheets of plastic covered the openings where windows and doors had been. A bulldozer had removed the old porch and carport. Out of these ruins rose a dining room, a breakfast room with bay windows, a den and a bathroom. And after fifty years of marriage I had a laundry room! The bay window will overlook beautiful gardens. To quote Mama, "The believing comes before the seeing."

Along with everything else, the attic had to be cleaned. More boxes came to light; some of them were marked "Miscellaneous." With Chris's help they found their way to the Salvation Army. Christmas decorations came down — we would be needing them soon; suitcases went back up — no travel for at least a month. We were too busy building.

There were times when delays and frustrations made us wish we had never begun, but Larry kept the plan before us. "We'll complete the job," he assured us.

God had given him a plan, a nail in a sure place, and the hammer was the will that nailed the plan to fulfillment.

At last the saws and hammers were laid aside. The trucks carried away the debris. The driveway's concrete was dry and the back steps had been transformed into a safe stoop with wide steps.

In the spring the flowers would come to cover the brown earth of winter. It was always so — spring follows winter, even the winter of the soul. I peered out my bay window and visualized a garden in bloom.

My dream of a Scandinavian kitchen became a reality too. Red checked curtains blend with blue gingham wallpaper. A scalloped white organdy eyelet valance, embroided with steaming white satin coffee pots and cups reminded us of our new friends, Rut and Bjorn Langmo, who had sent this gift from Norway.

Jan and Chris had a beautiful basket of soft blue and peach silk flowers arranged for our golden wedding anniversary. During the sheet rock dust storms, I carefully protected this treasure until the buffet in our new dining room was ready.

The furniture glistened
with lemon polish,
but when my guests sat down,
the sofa crackled and popped.

Now it was time to select paint, carpet, wallpaper and curtains. Limited finances and time made it imperative to find bargains — and find them fast!

With an "Onward Christian Soldiers" determination, the girls and I marched off to our war, pocketbooks swinging from our shoulders, car keys ready for action. This definitely was the day the Lord had made, and no one had better get in the way. Even trembling traffic lights turned green when we approached.

At one store we spotted the sign: WALLPAPER SALE! The magic word! And there it was, the color and the flowers that would match the basket arrangement perfectly. Within five minutes the wallpaper — on sale — was tucked into the trunk of the car.

Like three conquering generals, proud and ramrod straight, we marched into K mart and invaded the curtain department. We bought our rods and blinds, then "Onward Christian Soldiers" again. There was no time to waste.

J. C. Penney's department store had a sale on lace curtains. Once again the song of victory: The last curtains needed were in my safekeeping. Home we went and hung them in place.

"European lace?" someone asked, fingering the curtain panel gingerly.

It took all my integrity to answer, "No — on sale at Penney's."

For ten years I had kept the beautiful blue sofa, that our son Ralph had made, covered in plastic. Only for special occasions did the plastic come off. I cringe at the memory of the day I ushered celebrated guests into my spotless living room. The furniture glistened with lemon polish, but when my guests sat down, the sofa crackled and popped. I had forgotten to roll up the plastic and put it under the bed with the boxes.

There were still some purchases needed to finish our remodeling so Harold went one direction to get paint and brushes while the girls (Jan and Chris) and I went the other to the fabric center. Looking in the rear of the store for remnants, Janice spotted a bolt of material, another perfect match. "Mom, look. It's just right to cover that old chair and make a valance."

The salesman laughed. "Someone must be looking after you," he said. "Decorators spend days and weeks waiting for perfectly coordinated colors."

"Oh, He is," I answered confidently. "Believe me, He is!"

Harold gave the carpet man our colors and within fifteen minutes that purchase was settled. We had chosen soft beige carpet to match the walls. It would replace the gold carpet, stained and worn from years of faithful service. I almost gave a salute when the old gold rug was carried to its final destination: the dump truck. Gold has never been my favorite color.

The Jensen war on clutter was about to be won!

Now the laundry room. After having the washer in the kitchen competing with the coffee pot and telephone, I really thought a dedication service would be in order. Imagine: shelves for soap and a clothes bar to hang Harold's shirts on. It made me realize what I'd been missing. If I catch the shirts in time, I can skip the ironing, and my Norwegian conscience is quiet. And that is not all. In my laundry room, no one trips over the ironing board (when I do iron) and there's a specific place for the iron.

Larry caught me staring into space. His brows furrowed. "Is something wrong?" he asked.

How could I ever explain that I was remembering how I would run out to the clothesline to beat the black clouds of rain, and then drape soggy underwear over the doors inside?

* * *

It was time to prepare for Christmas! Harold had finished all the painting, and the furniture was in place. The plastic was off the blue sofa for good and Ralph's hand-carved table came out of a bedroom corner and stood in a place of honor.

59

The round mahogany table, Mama's wedding gift from the Jewish lady she served, the table I polished so carefully as a child, was given a prominent spot.

Above it hung Joyce Solveig's needlework of love for our anniversary:

> "I HAVE LOVED YOU
> WITH AN
> EVERLASTING
> LOVE."

The piano stayed where it had always been, and still was the focal point for all the family.

A place of honor had been bestowed on each piece of furniture that had endured years of living. Nothing was new, just restored. Then out came the old Christmas decorations and up went the tree. We trimmed the tree with the ornaments of fifty years, and each one held a memory. Carols, tree lights and candlelight all blended into the magic of Christmas.

We celebrated Christmas Day with dinner in the new dining room! A royal blue cloth from Denmark covered the table. Christmas dishes matched it and red candles were set in the white candelabra from Sweden.

The family pictures on the wall smiled with us as we gathered to ask God's blessing on this house and to thank Him for the gift of His love.

The music of "Silent Night, Holy Night" filled not only the room but also our hearts. It had been a long hard year of work, but today was a glad day of celebration.

"The beauty of a life is godliness and the beauty of a home is order." I heard that somewhere, and it has been tucked away in my heart. After fifty years of waiting, I finally have the room and order I have longed for. I have my place to write.

Order is a nail in a sure place and gives the mind a rest from clutter and the freedom to stretch.

A quiet peace fills the rooms, and I am conscious that every good and perfect gift comes from above and that God uses our hands to extend those gifts to others.

Order is a nail in a sure place and gives the mind a rest from clutter and the freedom to stretch as far as the ocean rolls to meet the sky.

Chad said it all. "Grammy's house small? No way! There's always room for us."

You are so right, Chad. It's the same house, the same street, the same yard with the gardens and flowers. Love just stretched the walls.

* * *

P. S. Dear Lord, just as we took the clutter out of the attic, help us take the clutter from the attic of our minds and bring order to our houses and homes.

House and marriage are still under construction.

THE BOXES

*I looked at the letter in my hand
and read once more:
"Our friendship is always there,
ready to be shared when the need arises."*

My office was beautiful. Soft peach and sea-green colors blended with the sand-colored carpet and papered walls. Behind louvered doors, Ralph had built shelves and closets for storage and a place to hide files and boxes. I planned to sort through the boxes later.

In the days following the remodeling, I kept racing from room to room. From office to laundry room, from dining room to kitchen. Everything seemed so perfect, so new. Everything matched.

"Jan, you won't believe it," I exclaimed in a phone conversation. "I took a sample of the shell wallpaper and coordinated the toilet paper, peach and green . . ."

"Oh, Mother," Jan wailed.

"Seriously, Jan, you will be impressed, and so will my friend Muriel. The toilet tissue matches the linens and wallpaper."

"And the sink, too?" she queried.

"That's not all. We found a perfect sofa that opens to a queen-sized bed, and I even matched the pillows and comforter. I hope you are impressed."

"Oh, I am, Mother. I am."

"You and Jud will be the first to have the honeymoon suite, and you can dedicate the peach bathroom. After all those towels we had, like Joseph's coat of many colors, I am pleased to announce that there's not one old towel in my new bathroom!"

Jan's long distance chuckle sounded close — and the sound was filled with her love.

* * *

Christmas passed too soon and the calendar relentlessly marched us past the happy season into a new year, ready or not. Such is the tyranny of time.

And so it came to pass that my lovely office was filled with boxes and papers. I must have looked ridiculous standing in the middle of the room, surrounded by my boxes, hands on my hips, dressed comfortably in my baggy red jogging suit with a big, handsome goose design stitched on the front.

"Going jogging?" someone asked.

I whirled around. Harold was framed in the doorway, scowling slightly. "You know I don't jog, dear," I answered.

"Then what on earth are you doing, Margaret?" he asked, his gaze moving quickly from box to box, then settling again on me. I knew instinctively that he really didn't appreciate my jogging suit, or the clutter.

I brushed protectively against the silly goose design on my sweat top. "Harold, dear, I'm sorting boxes."

He shook his head as if to say, "Still so many surprises after fifty years."

"Aren't those the same boxes we took from under the bed?"

I nodded and gulped. I already knew what was coming. He had that "no-nonsense" look, a pastoral gaze. "Margaret," he asked solemnly, "don't you remember that all those boxes marked 'Miscellaneous' were to be thrown out?"

"Oh, I remember. I'm emptying them."

"Then why do you have another empty box for the contents from 'Miscellaneous'?"

"I'm just looking over the mail."

"And reading it again?"

"Well . . . yes. You see, there are so many requests for prayer and I'm trying to remember if I prayed for them all. Then again, I happen to know there have been some wonderful answers and I'm not sure I stopped to say, 'Thank You, Lord.' "

"Margaret, you are supposed to be writing. I don't think Les Stobbe would appreciate you standing in this clutter when you have a nice desk for *writing*. You notice, I said writing, not rereading old letters."

"Les can't see me," I mumbled lamely.

"Maybe I'll tell him."

"In that case I'll put it in a book; he'll find out sooner or later."

Harold shook his head and sighed, "Please don't forget to mark your boxes." He was smiling now. "Do you remember when you packed our summer clothes in a box marked Christmas ornaments? We had to buy new swimming suits and shorts."

Oh, yes. I remembered.

He turned to leave. "By the way, what do you plan to write on those new boxes?"

"I'm marking them 'Answered Prayers.' If the prayers aren't answered by now, they will be. 'The believing comes before the seeing.' "

He shook his head as if to say, *Still so many surprises after fifty years*. Aloud he said, "You win. I'll come back at one o'clock and we'll go to Swensons for lunch. A fellow's not likely to get much lunch around here today. Besides those college waitresses always make fresh coffee for us."

"Before you leave, Harold, you don't really need to tell Jan about these boxes. You see, I promised her 'no boxes,' only 'properly filled ones.' " I hesitated when his brows arched. "At least they aren't under the bed."

With a chuckle he was off—Harold, my nail in a sure place. He knew me!

The office door closed and I heard the sound of his retreating footsteps. Then the slippered feet of memory walked gently through my mind as I read letter after letter. Finally I picked up one from my friend, Muriel Sandbo, and read it from start to finish. Her closing sentence touched me again: *Our friendship is always there, ready to be shared when the need arises. Love, Muriel.*

I held her letter in my hand, thinking back to the last time we met, when we unexpectedly boarded the same plane in Charlotte.

It was in April 1988, and the alarm clock had announced a new day at 4:30 A.M. With bags packed I was ready to catch the early flight to Charlotte, North Carolina, then on to Sault Ste. Marie. It would be a long day.

After a two-hour delay in Charlotte I moved with the crowd for boarding. Suddenly I heard Muriel Sandbo's familiar voice. "Margaret! Margaret Jensen!"

Our travels have taken us from east to west, north to south; but our hearts stay together. Today we were on our way to Detroit, where Muriel was to speak and I was to continue north.

On board, the gentleman next to me graciously exchanged seats with Muriel so we could talk, which we did nonstop for two hours. Our joys and sorrows mingled with tears and laughter while we shared our heart's desire, to walk in obedience to God.

"Do you remember . . . ?"

We remembered.

"Can you believe . . . ?"

We believed.

"You'll never know what I've been through."

We shared, and we prayed. We also knew that God was faithful. His word is true!

Before me stood a lovely lady, coordinated from her soft blonde hair to her matching shoes. In contrast, I stood limp and discouraged in my grocery-shopping grey jumper and nondescript blouse

---

It was time to go. We moved into the terminal, and then our paths had to part. Our hearts never moved. Friendship—that nail in a sure place!

Only half hearing the roar of the commuter plane that took me north, I remembered how we met back in 1984 when Muriel was a retreat speaker. My book, *First We Have Coffee,* had just been published. My starched cap and nurse's uniform had been folded away permanently. I had nursed my last patient.

But as a private duty nurse, that last case had been the most difficult. One day I cried out to God, "I can't stand this another day."

Like a summer breeze a gentle whisper spoke to

68

my weary spirit: "To the degree of agony will be the degree of ecstasy. This is your last case." I felt the quiet peace enfold me in God's blanket of love. Deep within, I had the assurance that God knew me by name, that I was safe in the hollow of His hand.

The case ended in December 1983. Then followed weeks of waiting for God's direction. The wait verses weighed heavily on me: "Wait on the Lord . . ."; "stand still and see . . ."; "they that wait upon the Lord shall renew their strength . . ."; "Fear thou not for I am with thee." They all kept returning, admonishing me to wait.

My precious daughter-in-law Chris insisted, "For you, Mother Jensen, 'wait' means to take a nap and be refreshed after a long hard case. But don't forget, Mom, Muriel Sandbo is the retreat speaker at church."

I had forgotten! I was too engulfed in seemingly unanswered prayer, forgetting that God's silence can also be His answer.

"Mom, hurry! You can make the second session." I did.

Before me stood a lovely lady, coordinated from her soft blonde hair to her matching shoes. In contrast, I stood limp and discouraged in my grocery-shopping grey jumper and nondescript blouse. My grey mood matched my grey hair. But she caught my attention and I listened.

After the meeting, we met. Suddenly I was enfolded in the warmth of understanding love, and her heart reached into mine. We both wept. She knew me though we had never met before. She had read *First We Have Coffee.*

"Get your rest now," she urged gently, "for the day will come when you won't know the meaning of the word."

For the next four years, notes, phone calls and rare visits kept us in touch. But today, on this bright April morning in 1988, God's love brought us together to remember a long-ago time.

The miles have been endless since that day, the road often rough and steep, but we had promises to keep. God always keeps His. I looked at the letter in my hand and read once more: "Our friendship is always there, ready to be shared when the need arises. Love, Muriel."

I reached for the new file, *Answered Prayer,* and slipped Muriel's letter under *S* for Sandbo.

* * *

P. S. Lord Jesus, dear Friend, thank You for the answers, and I give You this box. Tomorrow I'll empty another one. In fact, I'll bring them all to You. What a friend we have in You — all our sins and griefs and boxes to share. Thank You, Jesus.

THE LOST
LETTERS

*Although the years and miles come be-
tween old friends, the heart never moves.
God has those nails in a sure place to
keep the fabric of our relationships intact.*

T he shadows of the quiet evening stole through
the woods until the darkness settled outside my
office door. Somehow the day had slipped away
and I was still here in my office, sorting through
boxes. Old, seemingly lost letters, rolled up in
rubber bands, came out of nowhere and resisted unroll-
ing.

By now the stars were coming out and I still
chuckled over almost forgotten memories. I'll never
know why I made copies of the old letters to my friend,
Irene Steinhart. She has saved most of them throughout our forty-five years of friendship. "Someday I'll

publish them," she threatened.

"I guess we both enjoyed a good laugh at life's everyday comedies," I told her. "It certainly kept us from crying during the winter of the soul."

My friend "Steiny" can't travel much these days, but she dresses hundreds of dolls for Christmas and sends divinity fudge to Harold. And when our son Dan was critically ill forty-five years ago, it was Steiny who washed our clothes and sent Porter, her husband, with apple pies and sweet rolls.

In those early years, we walked with our baby buggies and debated whether we could spare a nickel for Prince Castle ice cream cones. We usually did!

Instead of playing golf, our men plowed and planted gardens. Then later, Steiny and I together filled our shelves with peaches, tomatoes and string beans.

On Saturday we packed a lunch, then gathered up the children and their playpens and headed for the forest preserves. Although the years and miles come between old friends, the heart never moves. God has those nails in a sure place to keep the fabric of our relationships intact. Laughter and tears are like a glue that mends the ragged edges, and no matter how far our children roam they'll hear the echo of the laughter of spring and remember the tears of winter. We all need each other.

One of my letters to Steiny read:

Dear Steiny,

Now wouldn't you think that Father's Day would be a nice, quiet, sentimental day? Nothing around here is quiet — sentimental, but not quiet!

We've had a severe heat wave, so I had to get up very early this morning to dig the potatoes for dinner. Not only the potatoes, but I also had to pick beans and then snap them. I baked a chocolate cake and made meatballs and lots of lemonade. Then we had breakfast!

Father Jensen took his time in the bathroom. In a few minutes he would be heading off to teach his Sunday school class, Bible in hand, smelling of Aqua Velva.

I caught the fragrance as he brushed a kiss on my cheek. "See you in church," he said. The car pulled out of the driveway moments later. With a limp wave, I returned to my duties: I cleaned the kitchen, made the bed and set the table for ten. If any extras came, the children would sit in the kitchen. That never made them too happy.

Then I headed for my allotted fifteen minutes to shower, dress, comb my hair, and add a touch of lipstick. That's why I ended up half-zipped. I was just too tired to reach around and make the home stretch. *Oh, well, I'll wear a jacket,* I thought. *It's cool in church.*

But then I couldn't find the deodorant, and I decided I couldn't face my beat-up Datsun to drive to church. The air conditioner only works in the winter.

So I did it, Steiny. I really did it! I stayed at home and turned on the TV. At least it was a Baptist preacher, Dr. Charles Stanley, just in case Papa was watching from the cloud of witnesses. I knew Mama would be shaking her head. Nothing would have kept her from church — certainly not a lack of deodorant.

73

Within minutes, so it seemed, I heard the car doors slam. I counted—no one had to sit in the kitchen. Ralph and his family, plus a friend or two.

Then came Father Jensen! "What in the world happened to you? I was worried sick." (I really thought that part was sweet—he was worried.) "It would be just like you, Margaret, to run out of gas on Sunday morning. Or worse yet, to get a speeding ticket." (Not so sweet after all.)

When I slipped into the aisle (with every head bowed and every eye closed), Harold whispered in my ear, "Getting saved, lady?"

By now, Steiny, I knew that I had committed the unpardonable sin. I tried to explain about the potatoes and snapping beans—and the deodorant.

I told Harold that the thought of standing, sitting, standing, sitting, and risking my half-zipped zipper showing, was just too much. And I dreaded the long invitation. Honest, Steiny, by the time they get to the ninth stanza of "Coming Home," I can only think of getting home to put the biscuits in the oven. By that time I would feel so "unsaved" that I should really go forward to repent for thinking of biscuits.

I remember what happened one time. I was to have sixteen for dinner and had to be at work for the 3-11 P.M. shift. (All the children sat in the kitchen. I didn't sit anyplace.) Well, that time I tried to slip out on the fourth stanza of "Just As I Am" so I could get the biscuits into the oven and fill the iced-tea glasses.

When I slipped into the aisle (with every head bowed and every eye closed), Harold whispered in my ear, "Getting saved, lady?" I started to shake from laughing on the inside; the preacher thought I was under conviction and decided to sing another stanza. I just bowed my head and didn't look up for anything, biscuits or no biscuits.

You can't imagine how hot it has been and we've all been praying for rain. Why can't they sing "Showers of Blessings" instead of "Heavenly Sunshine"? With all my zinnias wilting and all my corn drying up, more "Heavenly Sunshine" we don't need.

Oh, well, I finally got everyone around the table today. Harold still wasn't too happy so he asked Ralph to pray. Ralph was hungry and couldn't care less that I watched TV on Sunday morning. Besides Sarah was pounding her high chair and Eric whispered, "I love you, Grammy," before Ralph could say amen. (Eric had just spotted the chocolate cake.)

At least I did something right. I had a nice present for all the dads on Father's Day. The grocery store had a clearance table — everything at 99¢. Apparently the books titled *How to Be a Good Husband* hadn't sold too well. I bought three. They used to sell for $6.98, and you don't get a deal like that too often. I gave one to Harold and one to Ralph, and I'm saving one for Porter.

Maybe it was the timing, but the books didn't go over. Chris tried to cover for Ralph's scowl. She promised that she'd read the book to him. I can't tell about

Harold, though. I don't think he wants me to read anything to him right now.

That's not all. I lost Harold's Father's Day card. All I could find was a winter scene on a Christmas card; however, I wrote a beautiful poem on the back. He never saw it.

Anyhow, they all enjoyed the dinner and the chocolate cake. I went with Harold to the evening service. He held my hand and someone looked over and smiled. I smiled back. I couldn't tell that person that Harold was pinching me so I'd stay awake.

We sang "Just As I Am" again, but tonight I joined in with all my heart. I felt loved and safe in God's all-knowing heart—just as I am.

It turned out to be a good Father's Day after all, in spite of the unzipped zipper.

> Love from our house to your house,
> Margaret

I turned out the light and locked the door. The day had come to a close. Someday there would be a "Coming home, coming home, never more to roam," but for now I'll serve Him and love Him—just as I am.

* * *

And P. S. Until then, Lord, I'll be Your nail in a sure place, to my family, to my friends, and to any needy strangers You bring my way.

76

LONESOME TOWN

*I thanked God for the precious blood of
Jesus that cleanses us, our homes and
even a hotel room from sin.*

Outside, the rain drizzled drearily from the dismal sky, and an early morning mist shrouded the woods in a misty grey.

Inside, the coffee pot perked happily and my loaf of homemade bread stood on the breadboard waiting to be sliced and popped into the toaster. Real butter and strawberry jam would add the final touch. It was warm and cozy in the kitchen, and the coffee was good. Real cream helps!

When I opened my Bible, I noticed a date and a notation. Then scraps of paper fell out from the pages, notes I had written in airports and on planes. One was a reminder of my trip to Toronto, Canada in 1988:

It's a lonesome time tonight, I had written. The

aircraft came to a stop and I picked up my carry-on baggage and followed the crowd to Custom Services. One woman had forgotten her passport.

With my custom's slip filled out I waited in one of the endless lines where I watched multi-ethnic groups move stoically through slips of paper, translators and mountainous baggage. Their turbans and swirling garments added color and drama to the depressing routine of a long day.

Finally, I was out in the rain to pick a number for a cab. I was number 93. It would be a long wait.

Cab after cab filled up with people from various parts of the world. I felt alone and isolated. Few seemed to speak English. I was only across the border, yet I felt like a lone English speaker in an international crowd.

The rain kept up a bleak rhythm on the pavement as cabs pulled up to the curbside pools, splashing water on us. A weary cabby yelled, "Ninety-three," and I was hustled into his cab. The driver was from India and spoke little English. He was not interested in conversation so I settled back to watch the rain and listen to the swish of windshield wipers.

The Holiday Inn loomed ahead like a familiar friend. I wasn't in a foreign country after all, just across the border in Toronto.

I emptied my pouch of Canadian money on my lap. Two large bills. In my relief to get into the warmth and security of a familiar hotel, I tipped the silent Hindu a large amount. His thank-you sounded genuine, and I smiled and wished him a good evening in the rain.

After I checked in, I wheeled my own bags to the elevator to go to the eleventh floor. A convention was keeping the bellhops hopping and one old lady didn't look too impressive to them. Weary maybe, but not impressive.

I aired my musty room and placed my Bible, books and yellow pads on the table. I opened my luggage and found hangers for my clothes. The open drapes allowed me a full view of the city. Towering buildings seemed to melt into the thick fog and the lights from a Chinese restaurant blinked bravely from the street below.

In the middle of the night I awoke suddenly with a sense of evil in the room. Paralyzing fear gripped me! Was someone in my room?

Across the Trinity Square the walks and gardens blended into the grey mist while Holy Trinity Church kept a silent vigil. At times the Eaton Department Store peeped through the fog.

I watched the rain and thought of Harold. "It's a lonesome town tonight," I mused and decided to shake that lonesome feeling and head for the lounge and coffee shop.

The multi-cultural city of Toronto met me again in the lobby. I wondered if anyone spoke English. After wandering aimlessly through the shops I moved toward the coffee shop, where I was seated by the window. Again I listened to the rain, and I experienced that empty feeling of eating alone. I thought about my friends who had lost their mates. Tonight I could feel that barren lonesomeness that steals into your being like an uninvited guest and refuses to leave. I knew my loneliness would pass, but those friends faced empty years. I prayed for them.

It had been a long day with being up at 4:30 A.M. and the endless waiting in bustling terminals, customs and cabs; but now, the day had come to a close. Sleep was a welcomed friend.

In the middle of the night I awoke suddenly with a sense of evil in the room. Paralyzing fear gripped me! Was someone in my room? A dark foreboding cloud seemed to fill the room, and a frozen fear engulfed me. Deep within me I cried unto God, and I called out the name, "Jesus!" Then I jumped out of bed and turned on the light.

Nothing!

"We wrestle not against flesh and blood, but against principalities, against powers" that we can't see but can sense (Ephesians 6:12). Perhaps previous occupants had been involved in the dark powers of an unseen evil kingdom, I didn't know. This I did know: I was God's child, and the name of Jesus is greater than any other name.

I sang "Power in the Blood," and walked the floor offering praise to our God who is greater than all the universe. I took authority in the name of Jesus over any evil spirit that had been in the room.

The old hymns of the church came to me: "A Mighty Fortress Is Our God," " 'Tis So Sweet to Trust in Jesus," and "God Will Take Care of You."

I thanked God for the precious blood of Jesus that cleanses us, our homes and even a hotel room from sin. The living Word of God came alive as the wonderful words of life came to mind: "Lo, I am with you alway[s]" (Matthew 28:20); "I will never leave thee, nor forsake thee" (Hebrews 13:5). I drew new strength from the fact that in the name of Jesus we have the victory (1 Corinthians 15:57) and from my confession that "Jesus is the Lord in my life."

"Margaret, is there hope for him?"
"Oh, yes," I answered. "There is power
in the name of Jesus."

The room was filled with peace and a sense of God's presence. I picked up my Bible and then wrote on my yellow pad. After a little while I closed the Book, put down my pen and went to sleep. God's love covered me like a blanket, and in the morning I awoke to a new day of blue skies and sunshine.

A pleasant breakfast with Ralph Bradley, coordinator of the TV show, *100 Huntley Street,* set the day into full swing. The night of the misty rain and darkness had passed. For everything there is a season, even "Lonesome Town."

* * *

P. S. I was suddenly brought back into my cheerful kitchen of the present when the phone rang. I picked it up and a friend said, "Margaret, please pray! A young man who was in a drug rehabilitation program was brought to a class conducted in church. Trembling violently, he refused to go into the church. 'I can't! I can't! I sold my soul to the devil when I was in a rock group!' Oh, Margaret, is there hope for him?"

"Oh, yes," I answered. "There is power in the name of Jesus. There is no other name under heaven, given among men that can bring deliverance to this young man."

We prayed together over the telephone and God will use my friend to be that nail in a sure place, to give this young man someone who will hold him fast.

The unseen darkness around us is real, but so is

Amazing grace,
How sweet the sound.

THE PLAYHOUSE

*I remember last Sunday morning
when a packed church knelt in prayer
while the church bell tolled 23 times
in memory of the 23 million babies who
would never have a tea party on earth.*

T he Christmas decorations had been tucked safely away into the attic for another year. Harold was thumbing through some gardening catalogues, and I was looking out over my winter gardens, longing to get my hoe out and dig.

Mama's words echoed in my heart again: "When winter comes, the next thing to come is spring." Harold and I had seen robins–spring was surely on its way.

From my bay window, I could see the storage building that Harold ordered for our gardening equipment. I remembered the day it came. It began with a flourish–a cup of coffee and Chris, who came bouncing in from a car-pool. Then the storage building came, sliding in on rollers to be set under the oak tree in the far southwest corner of our large lot.

Now a storage shed was my idea of luxury, a place for fertilizer, seeds, flowerpots, shovels and hoes. No longer would I have to take my life in my hands trying to get around paint cans, brushes and plastic covers without falling over. My precious reserve of manure would finally have an honored place.

Harold cried, "Margaret! Do something!"

The 8' x 12' building was firmly secured. And the small window was right for a ruffled curtain. Mama would have been proud of me, curtaining the window in a "metal outhouse."

Harold put in a grass carpet and proceeded to build shelves for paint cans and brushes. I knew tillers, cultivators and a mower would soon fill the space.

Our plans whirled like sugar plums in our heads— until the girls arrived. Sarah, 10, and Kathryn, 7, exclaimed with delight, "Oh, Papa—a playhouse! When can you move your 'junk' out of our playhouse?"

Harold cried, "Margaret! Do something!"

I did! I moved the "junk" out of the playhouse and made temporary housing for gardening equipment elsewhere. Grass seed and manure were placed in boxes, hidden by rugs—out of sight, I thought.

A chest of drawers, a toy box and a window seat quickly found room beside a folding table and rusty metal chairs.

When the boys, Shawn and Eric, came to investigate the new management, a firm "wipe your feet" sent them running. "Grammy, the girls are taking over everything!"

And they had! Sarah had a one-room schoolhouse going, with paper and pencils, books and assignments all under way. When school was over the girls rang a bell, and it was time for tea.

A patio of old carpet had been laid outside the storage building. The folding table was set with a starched tablecloth, and a broken vase stuffed with weeds made the centerpiece.

Out of the attic had come old hats, and the cedar chest gave up bridesmaids' dresses of long ago. Veils, old furs and long gloves went with silver and gold slippers. Old beads and earrings had never enjoyed such prominence.

Sarah's flopping hat kept blowing in the wind. Kathryn tied hers down with a scarf. She didn't fool around with the wind.

Harold, too busy with other construction woes, didn't notice the new tenants—until he was invited for tea. Sarah, in a long dress and gloves, greeted her guests, a fur scarf dangling around her neck. Kathryn, evening dress and shawl trailing, climbed into her favorite lap. "Papa, when are you going to get Grammy's 'junk' out of our playhouse?" She had noticed the boxes.

Harold played his part well. After all it isn't every day you are invited to tea—Kool-Aid and crackers.

For everything there is a season. Now was the time for Kathryn's broom to sweep the patio, the time for Sarah's no-nonsense approach to education, and the time for the boys to complain that "the girls take over."

Somehow I knew that the "little house" would be filled with more than garden tools. Long after Harold and I are gone, the memories from the days of innocence will linger in the children's minds.

Wipe your feet seemed fitting, for the land of childhood is holy ground, a time when memories are made and stored so they can return down the years when the surrounding unholy ground becomes overwhelming.

The playhouse with jelly jars and glittering beads will all pass—too soon, too soon. The day will come when manure and fertilizer, hoes and shovels will take their place. But today, for such a time as this, let Kathryn sweep her walks and Sarah pour her tea, and by all means, let us wipe our feet.

I'm sitting in my office, remembering that spring will soon be here, and there will be more tea parties.

I also remember last Sunday morning when a packed church knelt in prayer while the church bell tolled 23 times in memory of the 23 million babies who would never have a tea party on earth.

* * *

P. S. Memories, too, are nails in a sure place.

THE BENDED KNEE

Scientists have lost God in the wonder of His creation, and theologians have lost God in the wonder of doctrine.

I t is good to be home. I don't have to pack a suitcase for two weeks now so I'm taking the time to look over the past calendar, read my journal notes, and reflect on the lessons I've learned from God's special people.

Today I opened my journal to July 1988.

It was 4:30 A.M. when my alarm announced a new day. I usually travel early because I have to catch an early flight to Charlotte in order to reach other destinations. I was wide awake when I buckled up in the familiar Piedmont aircraft that would take me to Charlotte. As soon as we were aloft I turned my attention to

87

the book *Five Silent Years of Corrie Ten Boom*. I walked with the author, Pamela Rosewell, through Corrie's later life: suitcases, airports, speaking, writing, people and mail. My heart cried out to know the faith and discipline of this great woman—Corrie Ten Boom. God truly had fastened one shining nail in a sure place.

I understood many of the things written about her because I, too, knew something about travel, airports, people and mail. Yet I sensed God was trying to tell me something else, to "be still and know that I am God."

How could I be still? Had my Bible reading and early morning time with the Lord become part of a routine? Was I marching into endless skirmishes of the day like a conquering general? I was thankful for health and strength to fulfill the endless tasks of writing, speaking and travel, but my calendar looked like a jigsaw puzzle with no empty places.

"Prepare for landing," sounded out over the loudspeaker. I tucked away my *Corrie* book and then autographed one of my own for the pilot to thank him for a pleasant flight. The title seemed right: *First Comes the Wind*. I wrote from Psalm 104:3, "God walks on the wind," when I signed my name.

After a thank-you to the attendants, I left the plane and maneuvered my way through the Chicago airport toward the baggage claim where my friend Grace Beezie would welcome me. God seems to provide a family for me in each part of the country. In Chicago, Grace and Bob were always there. Not only do they welcome me into their home and hearts, but they also continually welcome missionaries from around the world.

Suddenly—certainly without warning—I tripped and sprawled out on the concrete floor of the airport. A searing pain went through my knee. But wounded pride felt the sting, too.

Kind travelers helped me to my feet and with a thank-you to them I limped to a chair to catch my breath. I was in pain, but I could walk!

Stunned, I asked God, "Why? I'm Your child and the day began in Your hands. Now why this?"

I heard Corrie's voice through her books, "God has no problems, only plans."

My throbbing knee reminded me of how vulnerable we are and that without Christ we can do nothing.

"But this looks like a problem, Lord," I argued.

I continued slowly to the baggage claim area and picked up my bags. Grace was there to take me to the Moody Bible Institute where I was to co-host with Jim Warren on *Prime Time America*.

In a few moments we would be on the air. Jim prayed while Debbie Powell, his assistant, put ice on my knee. Faith and works go together. As Jim and I took our places I was still stunned by my helplessness.

The lights went on, the music played, and we were on the air. Across the miles, listeners heard the interview with George Verwer as he told how God was turning a tragic situation into triumph.

In the late 1950s George Verwer and a small group

of Bible college students had headed for Mexico in an old truck, packed with books and tracts. That mission fanned out with tents, sleeping bags, and hearts on fire with the good news of God's love for all the world.

George's dream, which had begun with the beat-up old truck, grew into Operation Mobilization, known as O.M. and by 1970 a 2,625-ton ship, *Logos,* was used for training nationals and transporting Christian workers from port to port for evangelization. Tourists by the hundreds visited the ship to hear the miraculous story.

For 18 years the *Logos* sailed, and it made more than 400 port visits, in 258 different ports, in 103 countries including Lebanon, Vietnam and China. At 11:55 P.M., on January 4, 1988, the ministry of the *Logos* came to a sudden, heartbreaking end. It ran aground off the coast of Chile.[1]

As I heard about the tragedy, it seemed to me that a great, shining nail had been pulled out, leaving a gaping hole of loss and emptiness. I almost forgot that God holds the hammer, and He doesn't leave empty, gaping holes.

George was smiling when he said, "The remarkable media coverage and resulting widespread expressions of sympathy and support from Christians around the world have shown us that God is opening a door which we need to step through in faith."

From seeming disaster God filled the empty place with an even larger ship, the *Logos II* — the work actual-

1   From *The Ship Called Logos,* by Elaine Rhoton, 1988, Moody Press.

ly had outgrown *Logos I* — and what God had done for *Logos I,* He would do for *Logos II.* It would sail from country to country to bring the message of God's love as its predecessor had done. "Not problems, but plans" came through again, loud and clear.

As I listened, my throbbing knee reminded me of how vulnerable we are and that without Christ we can do nothing. A fall or a grounded ship are accidents signaling that "the best is yet to be."

Just for me, Jim had one of my favorite hymns played:

> *"All hail the power of Jesus' name;*
> *Let angels prostrate fall."*

Believe me, I didn't look like an angel, prostrate on the airport floor, but deep within I cried out to bow to Him in humble adoration.

The *Logos I,* a nail in a sure place for all those years, carrying healing into faraway places, was now moving into a greater plan: a mighty iron stanchion in the structure of faith.

Jim Warren, using his creative talent, utilized news and voices from around the world to remind the listeners to "bring forth the mighty diadem, and crown Him Lord of all."

The next segment of the show was a personal interview with Sammy Tippit about his book, *The Prayer Factor.*

I almost forgot my throbbing knee while Jim asked questions and Sammy recounted amazing answers to prayers for young people in the Eastern bloc countries to surrender their lives to Jesus. Some of the older people had been praying for years.

Now Sammy has a dream of preaching the gospel in the Red Square of Russia. "The church begins to run on bureaucracy rather than on bended knee [there goes that knee again] when it refuses to wait on God."

Sammy recounted how he was arrested several times for preaching the message of salvation and how he used the living Word of God to reply to his captors. He continued, "God puts a great price on humility. We humble ourselves before God and wait for His direction. 'Be still and know.' "

I crumpled into my pillow. "I'm too old to be tramping all over the country," I whimpered. "I just want to go home."

I could nod in agreement. I certainly had a new sense of humility—gained from being sprawled out in front of hundreds of travelers.

Sammy rushed on, "The Holy Spirit, the school's headmaster, establishes our course of training. He gives us Professors Law and Failure as tutors. Professor Law teaches us the standard of God; Professor Failure teaches us that we cannot reach the standard. We are led to the startling fact that without Jesus we can do nothing."

How well I understood this radio program. I had all my plans laid out, yet one fall could result in my having to cancel every plan. I mentally checked the list—Pennsylvania; North Carolina; Oregon; Canada—

and maybe surgery and immobilization for weeks.

I had read an excerpt from Sammy's book in a newsletter Debbie gave me. His words now kept returning to me: "Waiting upon God recognizes two important truths from Scripture: the helplessness of man and the sufficiency of Christ. As we wait upon God we understand Jesus' words: 'Without me you can do nothing' " (John 15:5).

While the music played, I looked over the news release again and I read: "Prayer is more caught than taught."

I read more about this young dynamo in the release:

> Sammy has caught the spirit of prayer in places like Romania and India where God is moving in tremendous ways. These countries do not have the technology, the programs, or finances that we have in the Western world; however, phenomenal church growth has come about through prayer.

Jim Warren continued his questions. "But Sammy, what about the time factor? Our days are so full."

Sammy agreed. The time factor was one of the greatest hindrances to prayer. We almost forgot we were still on the air as we continued to remember times we earnestly prayed and saw great answers.

Then it was over, and Jim signed off the air. But our discussion continued.

The day came to an end and I painfully crawled up the stairs to the Beezies' guest room, feeling frightened and helpless. Of course I believed in prayer; but right now I was wondering how I would get home – or even get ready for bed. I thought about the miracles in India and Africa, but my knee was twice its normal size and I just wanted to be home so Harold could put me to bed or get me to our family doctor.

Grace brought another ice bag and I elevated my leg and said I was fine – until the door closed. Then I crumpled into my pillow. "I'm too old to be tramping all over the country," I whimpered. "I just want to go home." I ached all over.

"No problems – just plans," echoed in my heart. I reached for my Bible and read through my tears:

> Fear thou not; for I am with thee [if You are with me, why did I fall?]: be not dismayed; for I am thy God [quiet peace was slipping into my frightened places]: I will strengthen thee; yea, I will help thee, yea, I will uphold thee with the right hand of my righteousness (Isaiah 41:10).

I clutched my Bible closer and kept reading. I wondered if I would be clinging to these life-giving words if I hadn't fallen, or would I be sound asleep? Now I couldn't sleep, so I kept reading. Timothy and Titus, and then I walked through the hall of faith in Hebrews. Finally I came to James: "The prayer of faith shall save the sick, and the Lord shall raise him up" (5:15). I knew that Jim and Jean Warren were praying and that Grace had sent an S.O.S. to her prayer warrior mother. And here was James reminding me: "The effectual fervent prayer of [the righteous] availeth much" (5:16).

I kept reading. It was like holding on to a lifeline. I was afraid to let go of the promises of God. I put my finger on another verse and read: "If any of you lack wisdom, let him ask" (James 1:5).

"Oh, Lord," I cried out, "I'm asking You for wisdom to keep my priorities in order."

I slipped into 1 Peter: "For the eyes of the Lord are over the righteous, and his ears are open to their prayers" (3:12), and "Casting all your care upon him, for he careth for you" (5:7).

From out of the past I could almost see our godly friend, Mr. Mason — white hair framing his clear blue eyes — and hear the words, "Keep yourselves, little children, in the love of God. Don't move out from under the shadow of the Almighty. Stay close to Jesus."

I looked up from my Bible and prayed, "Oh, God, I know Your thoughts for me are for good. Did I need to be grounded for You to get my attention and for me to realize how frail I am without You? Have the cares of this world, the anxiety over my writing room, the endless delays and demands on time been choking out the living Word?"

Somewhere deep inside, I seemed to hear a gentle, "Yes." The study of the Word seemed to have replaced the feasting on the Word. I read someplace that scientists have lost God in the wonder of His creation, and theologians have lost God in the wonder of doctrine.

Mr. Mason is at home with the Lord now, but his life shone like a nail in a sure place, fastened by God, where the lonely travelers found a haven.

Corrie Ten Boom is at home with the Lord where the saints come marching in to sing the praises of God.

95

Mama and Papa have joined the heavenly throng—all of them God's special nails in a sure place.

Then today, Jim Warren, faithful servant, presented the news and views from around the world. To thousands of listeners he is that nail God has fastened in a sure place.

With my Bible closed now, I prayed for our faithful ministers, missionaries, loved ones and friends, people God had placed as nails in a sure place.

It was getting late and in the morning I was scheduled to speak to the 50th Class Reunion at the Norwegian American Hospital where I had trained as a nurse. I wondered for a moment how I would get there—but that was tomorrow. Tonight I needed sleep. Just before I put my Bible aside, I opened it once again, and I read:

> Now unto him that is able to keep you from falling [there it goes again—bended knees and falling], and to present you faultless before the presence of his glory with exceeding joy [oh, yes, Lord, I don't want You to be sorry You made me], to the only wise God our Saviour, be glory and majesty, dominion and power (Jude 24,25).

Good night, Jesus. We've had a long visit.

Now I lay me down to sleep—
I pray thee Lord my knee to keep. AMEN

* * *

P. S. He did!

96

THE
LOST FILE

Sometimes mere survival is our victory.

 arold was at my study door again. "Margaret, I certainly hope you get those boxes sorted one of these days." He nodded to the box in front of me. "What is that?"

"I just found a lost file. Remember how Grace showed me how to file the mail? Well, I got a little behind—like ten years. I've just found copies of letters I had written ages ago. Are you sure you don't want me to read them to you?"

He was sure! He backed away quickly.

I went back to my file. Mama used to say that we need a good laugh every day, then we wouldn't have to go to the doctor so often. I don't have time to go to the doctor, so I'll read these old letters.

"What's wrong with American families?" a TV host asked me one day.

I said, "We've lost our sense of humor."

Just as there is beauty all around us, so there is the joy of laughter from humor in everyday living. Tears can wash the eyes of faith so we can see God in the impossible. Laughter makes hope stretch like elastic to help us wait for the answers.

Janice used to say, "I can always tell when Mother is 'fighting the fight of faith.' Her letters are hilarious."

"What in the world are you cooking?"
"That smell? I just put manure
on the corn."
"Well, thank you, I'll take butter on mine."

Yes, sometimes we laugh together to keep from crying. God's Word speaks of joy: "Now the God of hope fill you with all joy and peace in believing" (Romans 15:13). God knows that happiness depends on happenings, but the joy of the Lord is of the spirit.

God fills us with all joy, while we are in the believing stage so we can wait for the seeing. If you can believe, you'll see the glory of the Lord.

Foolish jesting and idle conversation are not the marking of a Spirit-filled life; but the joy of the Lord rises like a fountain and takes away the cutting edge of the cares of this world.

I guess that's why I saved those zany letters — ones like this one:

Dearest Do,

Your letters are like a trip to the Orient. I've fallen in love with Japan, and, yes, I read *Shogun*. I didn't know we seem like barbarians to the gentle, disciplined Oriental.

Please, don't change, Do. When we five Tweten sisters get together I don't want you bowing and smiling. Don't you realize what effect that would have on our husbands?

The other day Harold walked in the door, sniffing and scowling. "What in the world are you cooking?"

"Oh, that smell? I just put manure on the corn."

"Well, thank you, I'll take butter on mine."

"Harold, you are not funny. I put manure on the corn*field*. The wind just happened to blow this way." I turned to face him. "Anyhow, supper is ready."

"In this smell?" He made his way toward the table. "By the way, Margaret, how long has the sprinkler been on?"

"I don't know. I'm just trying to soak the corn."

"That does it! You know as much about the economy as the Washington crowd. You put lime and fertilizer on your crop and run up the water bill. Then you only manage to get a few packages of corn to put in the freezer. You think you are beating the high cost of living." Harold shook his head sadly. "In reality, Margaret, you are the cause of inflation! Remember the strawberries? [How could I forget?] Not only did you spend every minute pulling weeds, you stood guard

99

against the robins. Then you bought a net for $15.00, and every time we picked a few berries we had to pull up the net and race the robins for the red ones. We ended up with the half-green berries while the robins sat in the tree and sang their waiting song."

I didn't answer. I just carried a serving dish of vegetables to the table.

Harold stole a glance my way. "Oh, well, honey, don't feel too bad. Look, I have a case of strawberries in the car. I picked 20 quarts at the berry farm today at 50¢ a box." But he was still on economy when he added, "At your price they cost $5.00 a box."

Harold had momentarily forgotten the manure. I hadn't. The wind was bringing it closer. "Let's shut off the sprinkler and go get a hamburger, Harold. We'll eat vegetables tomorrow."

It had been enough for one day!

The next evening, Sunday, was "Honor the Senior Citizens Day." If there is one thing Harold can't stand, it is being called a "Senior Citizen." "When I grew up there was no such foolishness as a generation gap," he told me.

Actually, he thinks he has to show an I.D. card.

The Senior Citizens were supposed to sit together in a roped off area. Harold would have none of it. Before we left the house he said, "I'll sit where I always sit." That is, where the young people sit. In fact, they are the kids who think they live at our house.

Someone made a nice speech and then asked the

Seniors to stand. I stood. Harold sat. Everyone clapped, and, of course, some Seniors were just making it "up" when it was time to sit down.

On the way home we stopped at the ice cream parlor and the young people made room for us. Harold told his jokes and we all had sundaes. Harold grabbed the check. That made the day for all of us.

Do, dear, it's now two weeks later, and such a dreary Monday, and I'm having trouble getting anything finished — it's such a nutty house.

Harold also said I was not funny, not funny at all! But Shawn and Eric thought it was great.

Your letters are so terrific. You should do a book, all about Japanese culture and art. Since you already know American culture, I can only fill you in on our hectic household. That book, no one needs!

One of the churches in town was having a "Wedding Day" at church. All the old and young couples were to march in together to the tune of the "Wedding March." We all lined up! The only problem was that we had our six-year-old Shawn and four-year-old Eric with us. I had forgotten about the Wedding Day. Down the aisle we went with our two young grandchildren in tow. As we passed an elderly deacon, I noticed his eyebrows go up.

I leaned down and whispered, "We belong to the new generation We take our children to our wedding."

The deacon didn't think it was funny. Come to think of it, he was right. Harold also said I was not funny, not funny at all! But Shawn and Eric thought it was great. They were the only kids to march to the wedding song.

Once we got past the deacon, the preacher gave a lovely talk on honor and obey and then we had to repeat the vows to each other. Eric and Shawn joined in.

"Now, you may kiss your bride!" the preacher said.

The young people saw their chance, and they went for it. Some of the older folks couldn't remember what to do. But Harold and I remembered! A good kiss and hug can set the record straight every time.

Like Shawn said, "I love going to church with Papa. We always stop at the ice cream parlor. After all, that's what 'Sundays' are for—sundaes!"

Your loving sis,
Margaret

* * *

P. S. Ten years have raced by since that letter to Doris. I just talked to her on the phone. She hasn't changed. We still laugh together, even over old letters. Humor is one of life's nails in a sure place. It helps us to "hang in there" just a little longer. Sometimes mere survival is our victory.

THE BOWL
OF CHERRIES

Nothing hurts like a broken relationship.

O ne of Jan's thoughtful gifts stands on a shelf in the den, a figurine of a pigtailed country girl sitting on a bench, holding a bowl of cherries.

Jan enjoys browsing through craft fairs and often comes up with gifts that depict the stories I tell. Beside the "cherry girl" stands a country girl with an old fashioned ironing board. It reminds us of when Mama said, "Ja, ja, Margaret; while you're dying, iron." Or how she said through the years, "Do something. Iron. It is a good cure for depression."

Again I looked at the little girl with her bowl of cherries. I touched it gently as my thoughts went back to a women's retreat in 1988.

* * *

Looking out of the plane window I saw houses, like small blocks standing in a row. Then as the plane descended, a church, park, school, and factory came closer into view. On a knoll stood a hospital overlooking parking lots and ribbons of highway traffic.

The plane bounced onto the runway, then slipped into place. Once again, for two hours, an airport terminal became my second home. I had to wait to catch the Northwest Shuttle to Sault Ste. Marie where Beth and Frank Venn met me and took me to their home.

The wind was cold outside the terminal and it was blowing hard across the Canadian border.

On the deserted highway, the deep midnight sky seemed to touch the treetops and I could almost reach the stars. The splendor of the Northern Lights hung like a curtain over the earth.

Frank stopped the car and we stood on the lonely road surrounded by frost-covered fields watching the glory of God's picture book. The heavens were declaring the glory of God to us; and we could sense the presence of the Word who became flesh and dwelt among us. There on the lonely road, we beheld both.

After a good night's rest in the home of the Venns, I was taken to Lake Superior State University where the women's retreat was held. I love these retreats and the women I meet. In each retreat I see the same expressions on the faces of beautiful women waiting to hear something that will uplift their spirits. I am overwhelmed, and I always remember, "Not by might . . . but by my spirit" (Zechariah 4:6).

104

As I looked out over this group of women, their expressions spoke of a hunger for God, a longing to know Him. They wanted His grace and strength for their time of need—and we are all needy people. These words came into my spirit: The Lord "is a rewarder of them that diligently seek him" (Hebrews 11:6). I knew God would meet their needs.

Satan tempts us in order to bring out the worst in us; God tests us to bring out the best.

My years of living had taught me about God's faithfulness through all generations. From a "living" epistle, my Norwegian Mama, I had "read" that "God's love never fails." Through my sometimes unreasonable father I learned unconditional love and forgiveness. God's ways don't always seem reasonable, but if we learn to obey seemingly unreasonable demands from an earthly Papa, we can learn to obey God, who (in our limited, finite thinking) doesn't always seem reasonable. God says give to receive, die to live, love your enemies and forgive—not too reasonable from man's point of view.

Across the country my theme had been, "I will fasten you as a nail in a sure place. Hang in there!" My message at Lake Superior was the same. Sometimes we feel like a crooked nail, a little rusty and hanging rather loose, but God says, "I've fastened you—hang in there." The trials of life will take care of the rust, a little pounding of faith will secure you, and the Holy Spirit, our guide, will straighten the crookedness.

105

Satan tempts us in order to bring out the worst in us; God tests us to bring out the best.

Sometimes that one lonely nail is the only hook to hang a hat on, or to hold two pieces of wood together, or a family, a business, a church or a society. Civilization depends on those nails, nails fastened in sure places.

Sometimes people around us can't reach God, but they can hang on to us until we can help them to God. I wanted to take all these young mothers in my arms and cushion their hurts, ease the sleepless nights or wipe up the spilled dreams like spilled milk. Too many of these women knew rejection. Too many of them were stumbling through halls of tears, looking for an open door.

With all the authority of God's promises and my years of walking with Him, I hid my tears of sympathy and offered instead a heart of compassion that brought them hope and new courage for tomorrow.

"You are God's special nail. Hang in there!" I told them.

Lined faces spoke of unshed tears and shattered dreams, of children who grew up too fast and got lost in a hostile world. I recognized them, for I, too, had been there. Out of the depth of a shared agony I spoke words of ecstasy, "God is able to do above all you can ask or think. God is not willing for you, your children, your marriage, or your relationships to perish. He came to save to the uttermost. The secret is to abide in Jesus, let His Word abide in you, then ask in His will.

106

"Are you a captive?" I asked them. Some of them nodded. "Jesus came to set the captive free – to open our blind eyes, to unstop our deaf ears and to give us a new heart and create a right spirit within us. We believe first, then we see!"

Scattered throughout the sea of faces were the wrinkled ones with white hair. They nodded confidently and smiled for they knew of God's faithfulness. They had remained that nail in a sure place. Then there were others who feared the tomorrows and grieved over the past.

"We are going home," I reminded them. "Our faces are turned to the lights of home. Together we must take the young ones by the hand and bring them home."

I shared the simplicity of Mama's faith and how she taught us the valuable lessons from everyday living. Then I told them about the lesson of the bowl of cherries (from *First We Have Coffee.)*

I took the women back with me to the long winter past, with its snowdrifts and blizzard winds. We sped from season to season until across the blue sky the white clouds floated lazily while the summer breeze blew over the Canadian prairie. It was that wonderful time of the year, I told them, the time of school and baseball.

I was ten and my friends were coming to play ball. I slipped quietly into the kitchen, in case Mama hadn't finished her talk with God. She had, and she had taken the younger children in the buggy to visit a neighbor.

Then I saw it – a bowl of cherries! Now I had never

seen cherries. I had seen apples with brown spots and oranges divided into six pieces. At Christmas we each had a whole apple and orange—only at Christmas. But now, here was a whole bowl of cherries!

When my friends arrived, I proudly passed around the bowl of cherries. My friends were also children of immigrants, and they had never seen cherries before, either.

When she looked at me I knew I had committed the unpardonable sin. I had made my Mama cry.

Suddenly I was holding the empty bowl—and I heard Mama coming home, singing, "'Tis so sweet to trust in Jesus." Then she saw the empty bowl. Her gaze met mine. I glanced quickly at the pantry door.

Mama kept a small red strap on the pantry door. She also had a jar of red pepper for a sassy tongue. When Mama put the red pepper on our tongue, we had to memorize a Scripture verse before we could get a drink of water. We didn't get by with "Jesus wept." Oh, no. Mama saw to that. We quickly learned to guard our tongue.

The red strap was for the other end. Sometimes we didn't wait. We just went to fetch the strap because Mama had eyes in front, back, and sideways. She always knew when we had done wrong. Punishment was swift and sure! She just had to look at the strap!

Now, Mama held the empty bowl. But she didn't

look at the strap. She looked at me. If only she had looked at the strap . . . when she looked at me I knew I had committed the unpardonable sin. I had made my Mama cry. Fortunately, Papa was away on a missionary journey. I probably wouldn't be here to tell the story if he had been home. He told us that God gave us His best angel to be our Mama and never must we make her cry. I was the eldest and supposed to be a good example. And now I had made my Mama cry!

The women in the audience were watching me intently as I went on. Some were smiling, some were afraid to smile.

Mama looked at me, I told them, and then she sat down in the rocking chair and threw her apron over her head. I ran! There was only one place to run to and that was the outhouse. I knew life was over. Never again would we Twetens laugh or sing or tell stories.

Mama sat in the rocking chair, holding the empty bowl. I have an idea she said something like this, "How is it Lord, that I am holding the empty bowl when I didn't eat the cherries? I only wanted to do something for my family. Life is like oatmeal most of the time, and then someone gave me cherries. I wanted to surprise the family. I didn't ask for anything for myself."

I also have an idea that that line of reasoning lasted only about a minute because I know Mama. She probably lifted up the empty bowl and said, "Fill my bowl, Lord, with Your love and forgiveness. Don't let the enemies—confusion, self-pity, resentment, and un-forgiveness—overtake me. Teach me Your way, Lord,

109

and help me to teach Margaret."

I just know she threw that apron down and got out of that rocking chair of self-pity.

In the meantime, I was in the outhouse. Now, I have news for you. You can't stay in an outhouse forever. Sooner or later you have to come out.

I also knew that I hurt so much inside that I couldn't live with the pain. I knew I had to go back to the kitchen, to the empty bowl of cherries. *Nothing ever gets solved in the outhouse.*

Nothing hurts like a broken relationship. Whatever the cost, the way back begins at the fork of the road where the relationship was broken.

Slowly I left the outhouse. The door seemed heavy on its hinges. It was so easy to run out there, but the road back was so long and so very slow. In my heart I sang my song:

> *Oh, Mama, Mama, won't you hold me?*
> *Hold me like you always do!*
> *Mama, Mama, please forgive me;*
> *Please, forgive and make it all new.*

Then she saw me. She didn't reach for the red strap on the pantry door. Mama reached for me.

"Oh, Mama, please forgive me," I cried. "I know you said pride goes before a fall, but I didn't know bragging and showing off could hurt so bad. If I live to be a hundred, I'll never brag or show off again."

"Ja, Margaret, it is good to come back to ask forgiveness. Ja, I forgive you, and now we ask God to forgive you." Her prayer was quick, simple. "Now, we make an apple pie. You cut out the brown spots and I'll roll out the crust. You see, all things work together for good. This could be one of life's valuable lessons."

I used to hate to cut out the brown spots, but this day I was happy to do it. Mama was singing again. The pie was in the oven and someone was coming for coffee. Through the years I have discovered that life has more apples with brown spots than cherries.

I looked at the dear women in front of me. Then I concluded with a plea to come out of the outhouse of unforgiveness, resentment, hurt, or guilt. I reminded them, "*Nothing gets solved in the outhouse.* God won't reach for the strap on the pantry door. He will reach for you for He says in His Word that He has loved us with an everlasting love. The fork of the road is the cross. Come on home!"

The retreat closed. Suitcases and farewells filled the reception hall. Ironically, the dessert was apple pie and someone called out, "We stayed up all night to cut out the brown spots. Someone took the cherries."

To the sound of laughter, I waved goodbye and was hurried off to prison — not to stay, but to speak!

THE PRISON

*No prison walls can shut out
the love of God.*

The prison walls loomed ahead like a formidable fortress. This was the place where my friends, Frank and Beth Venn visited regularly to reach out with love to "our boys."

Inside the prison, I watched the waiting room fill up with children, mothers and wives. Yet the noise level was subdued, the expressions serious.

Finally, I passed security (my hair pins kept the "beeper" going). Then we were led to the chapel.

In the quiet stillness, someone lit two candles beside the cross. A young prisoner played familiar hymns. Through my tear-filled eyes I envisioned a little boy practicing his piano lessons while his mother beamed with pride. *What happened,* I wondered, *between childhood and now?* He sat pale and quiet as he played.

113

Another prisoner stood to lead the singing.

> *Abide with me, fast falls the eventide;*
> *. . . In life, in death, O Lord, abide with me.*

A tall black man with a cap on his head stumbled through a written prayer. I knew it must have taken courage to stand before an audience, even to read a prayer. He looked like he would have been more at home on a basketball court.

Next came the prayer requests. A young inmate repeated the requests, while someone wrote the names down:

"Pray for my mom." A strong voice, earnest.

"Don't forget my kids." This man's voice was anxious.

A young man called out, "Pray for my grandma."

An older man said huskily, "Pray for my six sons."

I choked inwardly. Was he praying that his sons would not follow in his steps?

Haltingly the young man read the list—Joe's kids, Bill's grandma . . . a trembling voice called out, "My two-year-old son has . . . leukemia. Please pr . . ."

The next song was:

> *Just a closer walk with Thee,*
> *Grant it, Jesus, is my plea.*

The voices rolled in unison. I kept choking up. *Will I ever be able to speak?* I wondered.

Then suddenly I was being introduced, "Today we have a storyteller, Margaret Jensen."

I went forward and turned to face my audience. I could see their faces, the expressions in their eyes as they focused on me.

"It looks like I could be everyone's grandma," I began, "so I'll just adopt you all."

There was a quick applause — the sound of acceptance.

I told them about the little house in Canada, about the outhouse with curtains, and how I pulled my sled to get groceries cheap, including the dog bones for soup. I told how we Twetens ate oatmeal three times a day and divided an orange into six pieces.

God won't reach for the strap on the pantry door. He will reach for you because He loves you and is ready to forgive you.

A ripple of laughter made me know I had my adopted children. Then I told them about the bowl of cherries, and that nothing hurts like broken relationships. Even a king — King David — found himself in the outhouse. He had everything, but sin blotted out the smile of God and he, too, hid in the outhouse of regret and despair.

"Create in me a clean heart O, God," he cried, "and renew a right spirit within me . . . restore unto me the joy of thy salvation!" (Psalm 51:10,12).

Even a king couldn't live with a broken relationship with God. He found himself in a prison of regret.

115

Nothing gets solved in the outhouse. We have to come back to the fork in the road.

They were watching me intently when I said, "The fork of the road is the cross where Jesus stretched out His arms of love for *you.*"

When I sang, "Father, Father, please forgive me," some of them wept. I continued, "God won't reach for the strap on the pantry door. He will reach for you because He loves you and is ready to forgive you. Come on home! We can all begin again at the foot of the cross. 'There's room at the cross for you. Though millions have come, there's still room for one . . .'"

When I sat down, a visiting black preacher stood and picked up the theme. He told about his own Mama who prayed for her nine children, but one of them wouldn't listen. One day, sick and dying, he did listen. Eventually, all Mama's nine children came home.

The prisoners began coming to the altar, black and white, with arms around one another. We wept together while we prayed.

The black preacher hugged me, and I hugged everyone goodbye. *My boys. My adopted boys.*

God's Spirit would do the rest. God had fastened nails like Chuck Colson, like my new friends Frank and Beth, and hundreds of others, all in sure places. No prison walls can shut out the love of God, and God's power keeps those nails in place.

* * *

It was time to go home! Saying goodbye to old and

116

new friends reminds us that "when we all get to heaven, what a day of rejoicing that will be."

The roar of the commuter plane mingled with the sounds of snapping seat belts and flight instructions. I watched the sun in the distance rise gently over the frost-covered fields, then burst boldly into a glorious new day. The frosted icing on the fields faded as the sun splashed its gold over the blue waters of the North.

Finger islands seemed to reach into the lakes to clutch at the mysteries of a long-ago time when Indians in canoes skimmed the waters and fur-clad hunters grasped the fringes of the land. Then the soldiers came, and with them, silence.

Across the back roads of my mind I pictured the snow falling over the bridge that unites Canada and the United States of America, a reminder of God's love covering us all with a blanket of cleansing forgiveness.

Just as the bridge brings two friendly nations together, so faith links the visible and the invisible world. Just as the bridge supports the travelers on their journey, so faith supports us in this journey of life. Through faith, the weak are made strong; therefore, the trials of our faith are precious. The crises of life reveal that faith.

I marvel at the grace of God, that the same message of forgiving love can reach into the hearts of two entirely different audiences: the women at the retreat and the lonely men in prison.

At one time or another we all hide under the apron of disappointment or we run to the outhouse to hide

117

from broken relationships. One step of faith can take us out of the outhouse of bitterness, resentment, unforgiveness and guilt. Whether a child or a king, the pain is the same. We can't live with the hurting inside. We all have to go back to the fork of the road.

Pride will have its moment in the sun, then the glory passes and the cloud settles in. We have to go to the cross, for it is *at the cross where the burdens roll away*.

Oswald Chambers says: "Across the path of unholy man stands the towering Andes of divine righteousness no sinner can climb."

The guilty one asks: "What can wash away my sin?"

The answer echoes from the heart of God, "Nothing but the blood of Jesus."

The way of the cross leads home.

* * *

P. S. I look at my cherry-girl figurine on the shelf. I know I will be telling the story again in this new year. Once again I will pack my suitcase, and then see the upturned faces of people waiting—not for me, but waiting for God to meet them.

So "touch your people once again, oh, Lord, and pour refreshing showers on our thirsty land. We wait for You."

THE PERIWINKLE

God always has a centerpiece when He has His "periwinkle people."

rom my office window I watched the sun gently spread its warmth over the barren ground of winter. Then I looked at the work at hand. Surrounded by yellow tablets and pens, I knew I had to stay behind my desk.

But four hours later I couldn't resist exchanging my pen for a hoe. I donned my red jogging suit with the handsome big goose, and bent to the task of preparing a bed for my bulbs. Dry leaves, weeds and branches had to go. The earth was shoveled, and raked to make a soft bed, and then the rows were scooped out for the tulip bulbs.

It seems to me that the preparation of the ground

119

always takes longer than the planting. And the watering and weeding are endless. But when I see those red, yellow, and purple tulips stand in a row like picket fences, I know I'll do it all again next year.

Their bright faces welcome the spring. Then they retreat for another year, so much like some people I know—beautiful, bright and shining, for a season.

I give the same loving care to my rose bushes, trimming, cultivating, pampering, because when the roses bloom, the air is fragrant with their loveliness. The buds turn slowly into a burst of color making my rose garden a rare treasure, one to be tended carefully.

Again, my roses remind me of people. Aristocratic, elegant, charming and poised, God's rose garden of special people bring fragrance and loveliness to a sordid world. (I could envy them.)

Then there is the periwinkle, my kind of flower. They spring up with a zest for living, pushing aside the weeds with sheer will, popping up their happy faces of pink, blue or white. They border the ugly places and fill in the barren spots. I can plant them or transplant them, in sun or shadow. It doesn't matter; they just keep on smiling.

When the wind blows cold the periwinkles dig their roots into the soil. When the hot winds of summer blow they wait patiently for rain. When other flowers droop in the heat of summer I can always make a centerpiece with my faithful periwinkles. When the winds of winter come again, they are the last to run for cover.

As I knelt in the garden, I remembered my morning reading in Jeremiah: "When I planted you, I chose my seed carefully—the very best" (Jeremiah 2:21, TLB).

I kept hoeing and pulling weeds, and I remembered once again that God plants people, just like I plant my flowers. God plants the tulip people for a season. He plants the rose people to bring fragrance and beauty. Then what about the ordinary, the periwinkle people? He plants them too, because, just like me, He sometimes needs a centerpiece when others wilt. They are gentle, special people, nails in a sure place, and they have learned to HANG IN THERE.

Across Canadian and American borders I have met the beautiful "nails"—one in a wheel chair operating a successful bookstore on the prairie. From Alaska I met a young wife, whose husband had been killed. She brought triumph out of despair.

On the West Coast I watched Uncle Carl, in his eighties, living alone in the house he had built, fishing in the lake he scooped out and stocked with fish. I loved his stories of gold mining in Alaska, close encounters with bears, and walking where no man had ever walked. His tales could make an award-winning movie. Uncle Carl said, "I stand on the porch and listen to the wind through the forest. I hear the song of birds. The sun is warm on my face. How good to be alive!" His eyes have been blind since his youth, but he sees the world with his heart.

God's special nails are also in strange places. In Buffalo, New York, I was checking the bus schedule to

Niagara, Canada. A friendly cab driver came to me, "Hey, Lady, the bus won't be here for an hour, and then you'll have to take a cab from there. I can take you to the hotel and give you a scenic tour of Niagara Falls as well."

"With a pitch like that, you win," I told him as I climbed into the back seat. The cab took off and my adventure with Joe began.

"I love my job, lady," he called over his shoulder. "I meet people from other countries and get a real education. Can't beat that."

> *"To be loved and forgiven is better*
> *than winning the lottery.*
> *You tell those women that!"*

I marveled at how he maneuvered the cab in and out of traffic as easily as I weaved my way around my garden.

"What do you do? Are you on a visit or business?" he continued.

"I'm a writer, a speaker. I'm speaking at a retreat to about six hundred women, many of them from Jamaica."

"Hey, that's okay. What do you tell them?"

"I tell them that God loves them and has a plan for each life."

"Yeah? Whaddaya know! That's terrific! Ever hear about that guy in the Bible who took all that was coming to him, and blew it? He really blew it! Well, lady, that's my story. I blew it! You know something? My old man was waiting for me. He was there, and he took me in, fed me and took care of me — oh boy, was I sick! But my dad took me in. You know something? To be loved and forgiven is better than winning the lottery. You tell those women that!"

I promised I would, and I did.

On the way to the hotel from the falls Joe said, "I'm taking my little girl to Disney World. She'll be fourteen and that's my present to her." He edged the cab to the curb. "Here we are, Lady. I'll see to it that you get to your room. Those jokers better take care of you. I can tell you're a special lady."

When I paid the fare, I added a generous gift. "Something extra for your trip," I told him.

"Oh, you don't really have to do that, no kidding, you really don't. Hey, I know a good pizza place. I'll take you to lunch — my treat. Honest."

I wanted to go — I really did! (No kidding!) But, reluctantly, I had to decline. I had to get ready for a meeting.

With a "God bless you" I promised to send him some of my books, and a special one autographed for his daughter's fourteenth birthday.

As we parted, he grinned and said, "Don't forget what I said — to be loved and forgiven is better than winning the lottery. You tell the ladies that."

Across the miles I meet the special people who

bloom where they are planted, and who hang in there where they have been fastened.

* * *

P. S. God always has a centerpiece when He has His "periwinkle people."

TEN BUSHELS
OF CORN

*Life is what happens to you while you are
making other plans.*

I finally learned my lesson about planting corn.
The way I did it, each ear of corn cost about $2.00.
"Leave it to the experts," was Harold's advice.
So I backed my wounded pride into a corner and
turned my attention to the flower garden.

One day our son Ralph came over with this great
news, "Mr. G has a wonderful garden and we can buy
corn from him. How much should I get?"

"Just get all he can spare," I answered. Then
Ralph was off. I should have been a little more conser-
vative.

I had almost forgotten the whole incident until I
found my copy of another one of those crazy letters I'd

written to my friend Steiny.

7-10-1980

Dear Steiny,

Hope everyone is fine in your family. Our routine sounds like the "Beverly Hillbillies." I didn't have any better sense than to tell Ralph to get all the corn Mr. G could spare.

Guess what? He came home with a truckload — *ten bushels* of corn.

It was Saturday and that meant we all had to get ready for Sunday.

While Shawn lay "wounded" on the grass, Sarah decided to do a striptease.

I called Chris and the gang came over. Harold had been painting in 100-degree heat so he had found a lounge chair under a tree and was clutching a cold piece of watermelon.

Then Ralph came with the corn! We set up a production line. The men shucked corn; Chris and I washed it, and Shawn cleaned off the silk. About then one-year-old Sarah got into the shed and helped herself to lime and fertilizer. We grabbed her before she ate any of it and washed her under the water hose.

The boys got into a fight over who cleaned the most corn, and then Shawn hurt his finger. He stretched out on the grass, like the athletes do, and waited for a stretcher to take him to the medical center. None came.

While Shawn lay "wounded" on the grass, Sarah decided to do a striptease. She wiggled out of her diaper and held up her shirt triumphantly to show her bare bottom. No one could stop to dress her. Eric turned on the garden hose and watered everyone, but not the garden.

Chris dumped the ears of corn in boiling water, then we iced them and into the bags they went. We ran out of ice! I ran out of room in the freezer. Chris jumped in the car, cleared space in her own freezer, and brought more ice. Having her live only a block away is wonderful!

But this was Sarah's day! She found the tomatoes and began tossing them, "Ball! Ball!" No one would catch. We caught her instead, but not before we were sliding in tomatoes. We managed to can the rest — nine quarts.

Sarah was still wired for action. She found the sugar bowl and managed to get up on the table to reach it. So between her tomato-juice bottom and sugar-baby top, we just had to throw her into the tub, but not before she dumped the hair shampoo. She was in her world — bubbles all over!

Clean and smiling she looked like an angel, fresh diaper and all. That is until she found a plum. We thought she was bleeding, but her happy smile gave her away.

Chris shouted, "Somebody get this child!" but no one wanted her.

Papa said, "Go to Gramma."

Gramma said, "Go to Papa."

Chris said, "Go to your sweet daddy."

Ralph said, "Can't you see I'm shucking corn? Go to your big brother Shawn."

Shawn held up his sore finger, holding her off.

Eric kept the hose going.

It took all of us, but we managed to fill the freezers with corn, can all the tomatoes, and clean up the kitchen by 10 P.M.

Sarah, usually in bed early, sat in the middle of the table, big as life, eating watermelon.

The children were given another "sloshing" and wore Papa's T-shirts. The boys wailed, "We want to spend the night."

Chris wanted a cup of coffee, and so did I.

By then, Sarah, thumb in her mouth, had her head on Ralph's shoulder. This had been her night out and she wasn't about to forget it.

Neither would we!

I read someplace that life is what happens to you while you are making other plans.

Believe me, Steiny, this was one day we didn't plan, but if you laugh as hard as we did (when it was over), perhaps it was in "The Plan." The whole day was just another reminder that out of all things, even ten bushels of corn, God works together for good. At least the freezer is full, and Sarah had her moment in the sun.

Love to all the family,
Margaret

* * *

P. S. Today, Sarah is ten years old and plays basketball with a ballet twist. She dresses in ribbons and lace for a piano recital, squeezes close to her Papa in church and rides up front to the family Sunday dinner.

"I just love Sundays," she announced happily the other day. "I love sitting around the dining room table, all crowded, and everybody talking at the same time. I just love it!"

Harold smiled at me and I answered from my heart, "So do I. So do I!"

THE JOURNAL

What we allow God to write in our hearts
will come out through our lives–and our
pens. We don't have the right to be heard
until we have heard from God.

I stood in front of the room at the writer's conference in Wheaton College where I was to do a workshop on "How to Keep a Journal."

The seats were filling rapidly and the sound of notebooks and pens joined with the happy greetings. As I began the class I said, "This ought to be quite a class, and believe me, we really need to open with prayer."

There was a quick shuffling of feet – then silence. I gave them one of Mama's Norwegian prayers: simple, sincere, straight from my heart.

My grin came with the amen as I admitted, "Someone said that there is a good article on how to keep a journal in a magazine. Read it. Then give it to me. You see, I don't even know how to keep a journal."

Some eyebrows went up but we all laughed, too. "I did keep a diary," I told them, "while I was in school. Mostly it was about the serious love affairs twelve-year-olds have, like who carried Mary's books and who liked John now. Scattered in the diary I had a few sentimental poems.

Papa held up two pairs of high button shoes, one black, one brown.
"Oh look, Margaret," he exclaimed, "we have shoes!" I shuddered!

"But a journal? For me it is an account of my journey of faith, my walk with God."

I went on to tell them that when life is rolling along smoothly, my journal is blank. Out of the depths of agony come the words of encouragement, the wonderful words of life.

There are times we can climb the highest mountain, and dream the impossible dream, but we don't learn too much on the mountain. We see a great view, a great dream, but we learn in the valley. That is when we write.

That is the time, in the valley, when the Word becomes the living Word and we jot down dates and events, or we mark a verse. Years later we read our notes again and our hearts rejoice.

All the way my Saviour leads me.
What have I to ask beside?

For me, my journal has become my books. From life's valuable lessons in Mama's kitchen came *First We Have Coffee*. One of those lessons, that of the high button shoes, never left me.

Out of the missionary barrel, Papa held up two pairs of high button shoes, one black, one brown. "Oh look, Margaret," he exclaimed, "we have shoes!"

I shuddered! Oxfords were in—high button shoes were out. Papa didn't know that. And Mama didn't think it was important.

Mama looked at the shoes, and she looked at me. "We prayed for shoes, Margaret, and God answered. Not the way you wanted, but He did supply the shoes." She pushed them toward me. "Now you wear your shoes with a thankful and humble heart. This could be one of life's most valuable lessons. [To Mama almost everything was one of life's most valuable lessons.] It is not so important what you have on your feet, Margaret, but it is important where the feet go."

Sixty years later I share the story.

Out of life's barrel come the high button shoes— the hurts, the rejections, the losses and heartbreak. It is not what happens, but how we wear the shoes, how we wear life's losses, and where we walk with God. God is able to take all the heartbreak that comes out of life's barrel and make something beautiful out of it.

My father said, "Wear the shoes."

I had no choice.

Mama said, "Wear your shoes with a thankful and humble heart."

Now I had a choice: how I would wear the shoes.

God's gift to me was the gift of salvation. For God so loved me, and I believed. What could I give God? Only my trust in the face of seemingly unanswered prayer.

---

*We must surrender to God
what we can't understand.*

I had to wear the shoes; that was not choice. But I could choose between wearing them with deep-seated rebellion or with a thankful and humble heart. I chose a thankful heart, and that was my gift to God.

To lift up my spirits, I made up a song. The words came from what was in my heart, and I added a simple tune.

> *Little girl, little girl*
> *With those high button shoes,*
> *Don't cry anymore*
> *If they are not what you choose.*
> *Only remember that you are mine;*
> *Trust me, one step at a time.*

The years went by and we had our trials of faith — but then came the real agony, the dark winter of the soul, when our youngest son, Ralph rebelled against God's authority. Once again the pages in my Bible were marked with tears and notes, and my journal was full — pages of agony, crying out to God—then hope, encouragement, faith. Finally, the evidence of a son set free.

From that journal came the book, *Lena*. The letters and calls keep coming because I tried to give the same hope that I received.

Close to my heart are the people who have suffered rejection and broken relationships. Once again the valley leads to the Word, that living Word, and a new realization that we must surrender to God what we can't understand. We must love and forgive unconditionally.

In the love story, *First Comes the Wind,* the old Indian says to Lundy, "Lundy boy, lust can live with hate, but only love can live with forgiveness."

Papa's Place is a family journal where, in the valley, we all learned to sing "Amazing grace, how sweet the sound."

I continued, "Keep your journal, your walk of faith; record the lessons from life, and remember that faith hears the approaching footsteps of God's salvation. We can look back over that journey and sing, "He leadeth me — by His own hand He leadeth me."

Then there is another journal that is being written continually, the journal that God writes. We are epistles, "known and read of all men" (2 Corinthians 3:2). Not everyone will read our books, but everyone will read us.

Spurgeon once wrote:

> God writes with a pen that never blots,
> Speaks with a tongue that never slips,
> Acts with a hand that never fails.

What we allow God to write in our hearts will come out through our lives — and our pens. We don't have the right to be heard until we have heard from God.

Job cried out, "Oh that my words were written!"

(Job 19:23).

They are! "Though He slay me, yet will I trust in Him" (Job 13:15), and "I know that my redeemer liveth" (Job 19:25). Those are Job's words — nails in a sure place.

Out of the dungeon, fire and sword come the epistles of living faith.

> *Some through the waters, some through the flood,*
> *Some through the fire, but all through the blood.*

These are the epistles: the ones who are washed, cleansed, redeemed by the precious blood of Jesus, the ones who are searched and tried by the Spirit of God. These are the books men read: victory from defeat, hope from despair, comfort in sorrow, love in place of fear and hate. They emerge from the libraries of suffering, defeat, despair, sin and shame, to give the world *living books* to read, dramas of real life in Christ.

We still have great men, like Moses of old, leading nations through the Red Sea of unbelief to the Promised Land of the riches of God's grace.

Out of prisons and concentration camps come the Josephs, saying that men meant it for evil, but "God meant it unto good" (Genesis 50:20).

After breaking the heart of God, David could write, "Create in me a clean heart, O God" (Psalm 51:10). God called David "a man after mine own heart" (Acts 13:22). Both hearts had been broken. "The LORD is my shepherd" (Psalm 23:1) still sounds forth through the corridors of time with the endless promise, "And I will dwell in the house of the LORD for ever" (Psalm 23:6).

Broken people from all walks of life are dear to the heart of God. He writes tenderly on their cleansed hearts. All the world can read the script.

God writes with a pen that never blots across the hearts and faces of people who are in hidden places: the one who lovingly cares for an invalid mate; the Harvard scholar who works in the slums; the gentle nurse who gives her strength to those who have fallen by the wayside.

Then there are the fallen heroes, wounded in life's battles: the rejected lover who weeps for what might have been; the lonely widow who pours one cup of tea while she remembers her table set for ten; the young mother, suddenly forced to rear the children alone. They come from the libraries around the world those books that God's pen writes with loving hand in the lives of young and old, weak and strong. The world reads the smile of victory, the step of faith, the shoulder of courage, the hands in service, and the heart that loves.

> Fear thou not; for I am with thee: be not dismayed; for I am thy God: I will strengthen thee; yea, I will help thee; yea, I will uphold thee with the right hand of my righteousness (Isaiah 41:10).

* * *

P. S.
  You are God's journal,
      that book that someone needs to read.
  You are that nail that someone needs to hold on to.
  You are that seed that God has carefully selected.

19

THE PICTURES

*I could watch them grow up
before my eyes.*

argaret," Harold said, "please remember how I had to putty all the nail holes before I painted the walls."

How could I forget?

"Mother, please don't hang all the pictures you collected in fifty years," Jan begged, "not to mention all our baby pictures." She was trying to be firm but kind, her jaw set like her father's.

"Mother, we are all in our forties now! Do you realize that you have five pictures of me in your bedroom, besides those of the rest of the family?"

I had one behind the door I was thinking of adding. I don't think I will now.

Janice and her father were getting together on the

nail holes. They measured, used a ruler, checked with a carpenter's level, then hung the living room pictures. Perfect!

When Jan returned to Massachusetts, I waited for my moment. One day, while Harold was at breakfast at the White Front (a favorite place for hot biscuits, ham and eggs, and old friends), I took hammer in hand, squinted one eye, guessed at the spot and drove my nail in place. There, the picture was up. After all, this was my kitchen. I knew better than to touch the painted walls, but Harold need never know how many nail holes were hidden in the blue-checked wallpaper.

My gallery was kid-level, low enough for even the youngest to see. I had a collection of grandchildren any art gallery would envy. Baby pictures, their first day in school, and the birthday parties—all were there. I could watch them grow up before my eyes.

Then there was the pantry door! Names and measurements.

"Grammy, if you ever move, could you take this door with you?" one of the children asked.

"I guess we'd have to" I answered, "but we just plan to stay here until Jesus comes. Then it won't matter."

"You won't let Papa paint it?" another grandchild asked anxiously.

"Oh, no. Papa said that was one door he wouldn't paint."

"Good. Now Grammy, get the yardstick and see

how much I've grown."

The marks were there: the dates and height, even the weight. The pantry door kept the record.

The pictures and records could be destroyed, but the recordings on our hearts could never be erased.

At that moment I could only think of
your mother frosting her hair
(instead of a cake) and how
in the rain her hair turned green.

There was the picture of Janice Dawn, born when the dawn came up over a Chicago skyscraper, our first child, God's gift of joy. Her baby picture with a bow pasted on her head blended with the next, her mischievous face and twisted suspenders holding up her skirt. I chuckled happily every time I saw that bewitching smile. Then came the cap and gown. Then the wedding dress and veil ("Sunrise, sunset; swiftly go the years"), and they were two: Jan and Jud Carlberg. Now they are four with their Heather and Chad.

One of my unsorted boxes holds cards and letters from Jan that found their way across the miles, letters of love, thanksgiving, encouragement, and humor—all from a heart that remained "at home."

To extended family and friends, Jan's love knew no limits. To Harold and me, she was our little girl, brimming over with the joy of living and melting hearts with her love.

Then one day we heard her teach a large Bible

study group. Our "little girl" didn't belong to us after all; she belonged to God and was given for ministry. She was His seed, carefully selected, and we had been allowed to have that seed in our garden to nourish and to water, but not to keep.

She was part of the "ecstasy" in answer to some of the "agonies" of our life. While we nourished our Jan, Bob and Helen Carlberg nourished their "Jud seed" in their garden. Now both Jan and Jud belong to God — and the world.

In the wallpapered guest room, Heather's smile reaches all the way across, pictures from baby days to college. This special seed, so lovingly nourished and watered, was given to Ecuador with a medical mission team. She grew up with warm showers and hair dryers, but she has learned to bathe in cold river waters and sleep in huts.

"Grammy, I even learned to pull teeth," she told me. I didn't share her excitement about on-the-field dentistry but I deeply admired and loved her goals, her commitment and her growing maturity.

The guest room is reserved for Heather and her friends. From my "lost file" I pulled a copy of a letter I had written to her when she was twelve.

Sept. 13, 1977

Dearest Heather,

If I could only think of something uplifting to say, believe me, I would say it.

But here I am, and yesterday was another Monday

morning, and I went to the store to look for velvet for a skirt for your mother. I visited the French Room to get ideas for my sewing.

Wouldn't you know? I couldn't find a thing. Then I saw Mrs. Jones, rich, elegant, poised, and a victorious Christian. Believe me, she was getting the royal treatment — three salesgirls.

I knew she would ask me about my adorable children. At that moment I could only think of your mother frosting her hair (instead of a cake) and how in the rain her hair turned green. My only granddaughter has cold feet in the summer and wears socks to bed. Your adorable cousins popped bubble gum right after the benediction, like their own special "praise the Lord" offering.

Sunday, your great aunts were guests at church. Then we had a Southern "dinner on the grounds." We were attempting to be dignified, but your cousin Shawn went streaking through the line of legs to be first, and Eric hollered "Papa" so loud that everyone turned. Including Papa.

Just then the preacher announced, "All children with their parents!" And I stood there wondering, *How come I end up with everyone's kids?*

Eric, your two-year-old cousin, thought the meat loaf was chocolate cake and cried when he took a bite. (I hope the person who made it wasn't behind me in line.)

Your Great Aunt Doris told me how her two-year-old grandson eats like a man, napkin and all. I looked at Eric. He had found the chocolate cake, but no napkin. No fork. No spoon.

Oh, well, that was Sunday, and now it was Monday and I was in the French Room. I had on my old shoes because my toe hurt.

A stranger said, "You are losing your earring."

I smiled a weak "thank you." How could I tell her it was oily cotton (for my earache) that was coming out of my ear? Besides that, I was itching all over from poison ivy!

Oh, dear, I thought. *I just can't meet Mrs. Jones now. She looks like the "Stand up, stand up for Jesus" type and I just want to sit down. My toe hurts!*

I eased along behind the evening gowns, through the velvet curtains into the robes and nightgown section. I felt more at home with underwear. I know I should have been a glowing, victorious, witnessing Christian, but I was in too much misery.

I hurried out to the parking lot and got in my car, ate a banana for lunch, went home, got the clothes off the line, put ear drops in my ear and calamine lotion on the itch, kicked off my old shoes and got into my starched uniform for the 3-11 P.M. nursing shift at the hospital.

I looked like Florence Nightingale dug up from the grave.

That was on Monday, yesterday. Today, Tuesday morning, came and I decided to look for that velvet again. And as I was shopping, I talked to Jesus. Out loud? Yes, of course. You know something, Heather?

144

Jesus and I can talk like old friends. Usually I do most of the talking. This time I told Him about my toe and the victorious Mrs. Jones and about the itching and all the things I have to do.

He listened.

Then I got quiet and stopped talking, and you know something? He talked back to me, so gentle and kind.

"Margaret," He said, "your toe is better this morning and your ear doesn't hurt and the itching is gone. It's going to be a good day. After all, I made it. I'll even help you find the velvet. I love your kooky family [I really think He said kooky], chocolate cake, bubble gum and all."

The angels laughed at your mother's green hair and your socks in bed in the summertime. And Jesus reminded me, "I'm with you at all times." Then He asked, "But do you have to hide Me in the underwear department? You know, I love you—just like you are."

Anyhow, that's how it all sounded to me, and I answered back, "You know something, Jesus? I love You too."

Love to all,
Grammy

* * *

I know the box of letters and pictures could be destroyed, but the engravings in my heart can never be lost. God can't lose us either; we are engraved in His hand and His heart.

145

When I walk into the den, with the morning sun streaming through the windows, the first face I meet is number one grandson, Chad. His creative self-portrait looks at me with somber eyes that let me know how deeply he thinks — even when his humor and laughter fill the house. A zest for life keeps him in perpetual motion.

"I don't think that's funny, Eric. We don't want Grammy to die."

When very young, he listened to his mother sing a lullaby, then instructed her, "Mama, don't sing the baby songs. Sing 'How Great Thou Art.' "

In this frightening world we all need a big God!

My breakfast room is another pictorial review. I can hear Harold again, "Margaret, we really don't need wallpaper in here. A world map covers one wall and your little Scripture plaques cover the other." Then he stared at the window. "Why are all those hearts in the window?"

I had to take some of them down. But which ones? The little wooden, handpainted ones? The lacy embroidered ones? Those with precious Norwegian or Swedish messages on them? All little love gifts from old and new friends, each hanging like a Christmas ornament on a ribbon tacked to the upper frame. I finally made my agonizing choices. I guess there is a limit to everything.

The world map is low enough for the young ones to see. They can pinpoint Ecuador where their cousin

146

Heather went. They can point out Spain where the Teppers work with drug addicts. Then there's Norway, England, Denmark, Sweden and Germany, where their ancestors came from. The world becomes part of our world; and the missionaries, people like us, are located in real places.

Then there's the old worn plaque: "Home Sweet Home, where each lives for the other and all live for God." A great missionary statesman, T. J. Bach, gave that plaque to us forty-five years ago. It stays. Harold agrees.

Another plaque, "All things work together for good," is done in blue embroidery to match the kitchen. It hangs under the clock, a reminder that our times are in His hands.

I gaze around at the other messages in the kitchen and my heart responds: "Love never fails"; "God Bless You"; "I Love You"; "Velkommen," a Norwegian blessing . . .

Now, I ask you, which one should come down? I say none.

On the dining room wall, pictures of Jan, Dan and Ralph look at me with eyes of wonder. The pictures were taken when each one was sixteen, and saw the world through eyes full of adventure. They smile at us here; after all it was at this same table they were nourished, and still are. When I walk through the rooms I talk to the Lord about each one and somehow I know God takes care of them.

Ralph, the youngest, whose feet once strayed into

a far country, had a heart that never left home. One day God miraculously brought the feet home. In time God gave him Christine, then added Shawn, Eric, Sarah, and Kathryn. Pictures of all of them smile from the dining room wall.

One day I found a note from a very young Eric.

> Dear Grama,
> I love you very much
> If you di I wil
> cry sorful ters
> Love, Eric

I also have a cup he painted. It has a house, with a rope reaching to the sky. On the rope was a figure like a trapeze artist.

"What is it?" (Now that was a mistake.)

"Grammy, that is you going to heaven."

Shawn interrupted, "I don't think that's funny, Eric. We don't want Grammy to die."

"Oh, I know that. I just want her to know that I know where she is going."

Heaven is real—even to the young.

One morning several years ago the phone rang, and Shawn's pitiful voice came across the line, "Come get me, Grammy; I'm having a hard day."

He was too young to walk over alone so I met him at his block. (He lived only a block away.) I watched that dejected little fellow coming down the street, head down, feet dragging.

We didn't talk about what went wrong. Instead,

we played games, sang songs and went to get hamburgers. It ended up as a good day.

I understood Shawn's hard day. How many times I couldn't pray, couldn't read, couldn't understand. In total desperation I just called to heaven, "God, come get me; I'm having a hard day." Gently, lovingly, He came. He didn't ask me what went wrong. He didn't point out my failures. He just covered me with understanding love. With God, I knew it would end up as a good day. It did!

On Sunday morning, the Jensen clan fills up a church pew—especially when Steve, our nephew, and Beverly, Benjamin and Paul sit with us. Harold makes certain that we are always on time. So early one Sunday morning, before church even began, Steve and his family slipped into our pew. Steve almost doubled up laughing when he greeted us, "You won't believe what happened to us this morning."

Immediately, his tone and expression caught our interest. We listened intently.

"We were rushing to get to Sunday school and we all landed in the bathroom at the same time. I was in the shower; Beverly was blow-drying her hair. Benjamin [five] was 'aiming' in the general direction and Paul [two] was standing in line. In desperation, Benjamin announced, 'There are four people in here. Will *one* please leave?' "

We laughed then, but I thought of all the times I could have cried when a houseful of relatives stood in line for our one bathroom.

No wonder I prize the beautiful second bathroom! Chris and I had picked the wallpaper. Harold painted. I waited for my moment to grab a hammer and nails.

One morning Chris (God's gift to all the family) looked at the new curtains and walls, and then turned to me. "Mom, did you *have* to put your embroidered 'Make a joyful noise' plaque in the bathroom?"

I nodded weakly, "It matches my towels."

* * *

P. S. Come to think of it, it matches the whole house.

It stays! Right where it is!

PARADE
OF ROSES

*I have come to realize that what Mama
said was true.*

When I look back over my calendar I stare in
awe at the wonder of God's grace.

Believe me, I remember that I am the
"chicken" who gets lost in the parking lot. I
am the grandma whose grandchildren say,
"Take us to the mall. We'll remember where you park."

For me to remember, I have to make a mental note
of *men's underwear exit* or *Christian Dior nightgowns.*
Nowadays, though, I don't have time to go to the mall.
I live in airplanes.

On one trip I spilled coffee all over me and all over
the man in seat B. As we mopped up the mess together
he sighed and said, "I'm glad I'm heading home, not

going to a meeting."

I mumbled, "So am I glad I'm heading home," and I thought, *especially with coffee on my white suit.*

With a burst of inspiration I reached into my attaché case and pulled out a copy of my book *First We Have Coffee.* He exploded with laughter as he accepted my gift and apology.

"You gotta be kidding," he said.

Later I received a note from him and his wife, thanking me for the book and hoping we'd meet again. But the note also said, "This time keep the coffee on your tray."

Is it any wonder Harold worries about me?

Five years ago, in response to my first invitation to speak in the West, I took my *solo flight* across country—the first time I traveled without Harold. I told you I was chicken. (Harold prays a lot.)

When the senior pastor of a large church, Owen Shackett, and his lovely wife Betty welcomed me to the Seatac Airport near Tacoma, Washington, they didn't know as they drove me to the hotel that the smiling author was really crying on the inside. But God knew! God knew that she had just finished her solo flight.

A bowl of fruit and lovely flowers with a note of welcome were sitting on the table in the hotel room. I knelt by the bed and just cried to the Lord. God's presence filled the room and His peace filled my heart. For without Him, I can do nothing. With Him, all things are possible.

The Shacketts and I enjoyed a wonderful time together. A special bond of friendship knit our hearts together. Open homes and open hearts are special nails in a sure place for those who travel many lonely miles. The dry springs are refreshed and the well is full again.

One place where I am always refreshed is at a nursing home in Gig Harbor, Washington. As we travel over the bridge to Gig Harbor, we pass the sailing boats and the quaint shops, and we view the distant mountains etched against blue skies. Then our car wends its way through a woods to a beautiful setting: the Cottesmore Nursing Home. There is nothing depressing here for it is Scandia Day, the 17th-of-May Norwegian celebration.

Inside the home, a large dining-reception area is decorated in red, white and blue. The front hall looks like a craft fair with art and creative work from different countries. Long tables bend under the traditional lefse and other Scandinavian delicacies, not to mention the wonderful aroma of coffee brewing, gallons of it.

Fiddlers in Scandinavian garb entertain the incoming crowd. Residents and guests in beautiful native costumes add flavor and color to the sound of music and laughter. Wheelchairs are rolled in and the feet of the elderly come alive again, tapping to the accordion polka.

Songs and stories bring the old and new together. And I, a happy Norwegian storyteller, am honored to be a part of it.

All this joyous celebration for the entire community was the dream of one vivacious woman, Inez Glass. Inez, an Air Force flight nurse in World War II, already had a concern for the elderly in her own family. She soon became involved in the care of the geriatric patients and as a result became committed to them. Her original plan to care for her own elderly family has since grown to the care of a community family of more than a hundred people.

The songs of the birds joined the organ music while down the aisle came missionaries from around the world, one by one, each carrying a rose.

In a world where the news depicts the plight of the elderly, highlighting stories of neglect and abuse, it is a miracle to see what one woman's dream can do.

Love and compassion envelops this lovely home for the elderly, and the entire community comes to celebrate Scandia Day. The heavens must rejoice at this shiny nail God has fastened in a sure place, and all the "nails" who work with her.

I look at my calendar, and May is marked again for Scandia Day.

* * *

The West has called me a number of times since then, and just last year I winged my way across the miles to the beautiful Garden Grove Crystal Cathedral in California for a major church convention. Coffee was served outside while hostesses in large flowered hats greeted the visitors. Women were streaming into the auditorium surrounded by beauty and music. The majestic organ pealed forth with such power it seemed that heaven and earth joined in praise to God.

The setting was spectacular: Singing birds and water fountains dancing in the sunlight blended with the music of the choirs.

I sat on the marble platform and marveled at the creativity that comes from God through His people. Then came the Parade of Roses!

The songs of the birds joined the organ music while down the aisle came missionaries from around the world, one by one, each carrying a rose.

My tears rolled.

As each missionary reached the platform, she gave her name, the country where she served, and a verse in the native tongue. Then she placed her rose in a beautiful vase.

They kept coming.

The newer missionaries who had served one or two terms; the older ones with some ten, twenty, thirty, and even forty years of mission living behind them.

I kept choking up.

The last missionary did it!

She marched with a sure tread, planted her rose with authority, gave her name and added, "I teach missionaries' kids, and my verse is, 'Give me five!' " — her verse in the "native tongue" of her field!

In response to David's request for "five" loaves in 1 Samuel 21:3, he was given hallowed bread. To this missionary, her young people were "hallowed bread" and she wanted all of us to understand that. She spoke in their language and they knew she understood them and loved them, and so did the rest of us. Applause filled the cathedral. I wiped my eyes and took a deep breath — I was next on the program.

I shared the story of the high button shoes, and Mama who said, "Ja, it is not so important what your feet wear; it is important where your feet go . . . ." Through the years I have come to realize that what Mama said was true: "It is one of life's valuable lessons."

God did not send His son to die for me just to give me shiny new shoes, but that my feet would walk in paths of righteousness.

Looking out over that vast audience, I saw not only the missionaries, but also all God's people who walk in paths of obedience. And I rejoiced, for in living color around the world they are God's special nails fastened in sure places.

THE CHOICE

*Character is the sum total of
all our everyday choices.*

I *shouldn't be thinking about gardening when I
have to write, but Harold keeps all those seed
catalogues around making my choices most difficult.* So, just for a few minutes, I went out to
check the bushes.

The red bush was putting out buds. The holly were
loaded with red berries. Now I'm looking for the crocus
bulbs to send their shoots through—a real sign of
spring.

And then it will get warmer and I'll be out there
bending over (and not on my knees) to dig up, plant, or
transplant, my garden.

One day Harold watched me. "Margaret, do you
realize the neighbors have never seen your face?" he
asked. So for Harold's sake, this spring I'll try to bend

my knees more.

That day when Harold worried about my bending was my kind of morning to plant or transplant. It was a drizzly, misty morning and I didn't have to drag the hose around. I was up very early, routine for me, confident that no one would see me in my shower cap (to keep my hair dry), my old pants with the loose elastic, and my muddy garden shoes.

Oh, I was happy that morning. I had my scooper and hoe, a bag of fertilizer, and all those wonderful plants to put in the bare spots.

It was the choice that got me: Either drop the plants or drop the pants.

The rain came harder and my shower cap came over my eyes. For the most part, my hair stayed dry, but the elastic in my old paint-pants didn't. I was determined to finish the planting, so I kept working.

Before long, Harold called to me. "Margaret, telephone. Long distance." Now that always gets me to the phone. But Harold says it even if Chris is calling from down the block.

It was still early. I figured it was my sister Doris. She's the only other one I know who gets up with the birds. As I turned to face Harold, he gave me an I-can't-believe-you look. He glared at my tilted shower cap and my sagging paint-pants. "The phone, Margaret," he reminded me.

I stood there with my hands full of muddy plants

and with my pants falling—staring back. "Who is it?"

He simply said, "Margaret, the phone. Drop the plants."

Drop the plants? I thought. *What does he know about transplanting? He stands there, clean and spotless, holding a cup of coffee. He doesn't know what it means to plant in the rain so you don't need to drag the hose around.* But my pants were falling. I elbowed the waist band to secure them.

"Margaret, drop the plants!" he called again between sips of coffee.

I heard him. It was the choice that got me: *Either drop the plants or drop the pants.*

I chose! I dropped the soft, wet, muddy plants, grabbed my pants, kicked off my shoes and rushed into the house to answer the phone.

It was Doris. She said she was praying for me—she usually does. I needed it this morning. So did my plants.

I told her it was the choices in life that were so difficult. She agreed, and then added, "The choices aren't always between good and evil; sometimes they're between good and best."

"I'll try to remember that," I promised.

A hot shower and a good breakfast ended my gardening for the day. It was still early, but now time to read God's directions for a new day. I read in my devotions that character is the sum total of our everyday choices. And I thought about Joseph in the Bible—he decided who he was before he decided what he would do. He lived out his choices.

Everyone around us is affected by the choices we make. Jesus says, "Come and learn," but we would rather "go and do."

God will not force His will upon us, but if we don't choose God's will, Satan will force *his* will upon us.

I remember the story Papa told about the farmer and the mule. The mule wouldn't move, no matter what the farmer did.

A bee came along and told the farmer, "I'll help you."

The farmer shook his head. "If I can't make that stubborn mule start plowing, how can you make him?"

"Oh, I can't make that mule go," the bee admitted, "but I sure can make him *willing* to go." The song says:

> *God never calls us to go 'gainst our will,*
> *But he just makes us willing to go.*

Sometimes it is hard to obey God—but it really is harder not to. God will take care of the consequences of our obedience to Him.

I turned to my favorite devotional, Oswald Chambers's *My Utmost for His Highest*.

> The warfare is not against sin. We can never fight sin. Jesus deals with sin in redemption. The conflict is along the line of turning our natural life into a spiritual life—done by a series of moral choices.

Jesus said, "Come, learn." We make the choice.

In May 1988 near Carrolton, Kentucky, a pickup truck going the wrong way on Interstate 71 crashed into a church bus, and 27 people were killed. During the funeral of the children who had died in that tragic accident one black woman stood up to sing, "I've come too far to turn back."

Although her heart was breaking for her son — she made the deliberate choice to obey, to sing, to not turn back.

Her child was in one of the caskets, but the mother had already chosen. "As for me, and my house, we will serve the LORD" (Joshua 24:15).

God had not forced this woman to sing. He did not force her to stay with a straight course. She had already learned the joy of obedience. Once again — although her heart was breaking for her son — she made the deliberate choice to obey, to sing, to not turn back. She would continue to trust the promises of God.

Her son would dwell in the house of the Lord forever because God had chosen to prepare a place for him. The woman was still growing, still learning to trust Jesus completely.

THE BLIZZARD

"The sun is shining on the other side."

It began on Friday, December 16, 1988, at 7 A.M. when my daughter-in-law Chris and I set out on a journey.

Harold packed the books and suitcases in the car, gave a friendly smile to us and then warned us to be careful about driving in the rain.

After prayer, Chris took the wheel and we turned toward highway 421, heading for Greensboro, North Carolina, a two-hundred-mile trip.

Our plans were to meet my sisters Grace and Doris for lunch at the K. & W. Cafeteria. Chris and I laughed and talked about how much fun it was to get away without the little ones. She was to meet her friend Peggy so the two of them could shop for last-minute Christmas bargains. I had my pen and paper so I could write in the quiet setting of the Hammer home. I was scheduled to be the guest speaker at the traditional Christmas breakfast at the Trinity Church on Saturday.

As we drove the rain kept coming down, but the windshield wipers kept visibility fairly good.

Then suddenly the rain turned to snow!

I realize that snow doesn't excite my friends in Canada too much, but one snowflake below the Mason-Dixon line brings our Southern world to a screeching halt.

> *"How deep is the snow, Doris?*
> *The breakfast isn't still on, is it?"*

We hit the panic button! Snowflakes the size of marshmallows were coming at us, splattering the windshield and covering the hood of the car. We pulled into a gas station for advice about the weather.

As the gas attendant filled a customer's tank, the customer listened to us and then shook his head. "Lord have mercy, ladies," he said, "y'all better be turning back, but fast. I been down the road a ways and it be worse—much worser than here. Y'all don't want to be out in no blizzard. You best turn back."

Chris shrugged, her expression obviously one of disappointment. But she nosed the car homeward.

Harold and Ralph were waiting. "Wow, are we glad to see you," Ralph said. "I guess the meeting has been called off. Must be a real blizzard in Greensboro. We never get snow like this. By the way, how bad is it in

Greensboro?"

"We don't know—we just turned back when the man at the gas station near Clinton told us it was worse down the road."

"You mean, you didn't call Doris?" Harold asked.

That's when Chris picked up the phone. "How deep is the snow, Doris? The breakfast isn't still on, is it?"

"There is no snow here, just beautiful sunshine. Of course the Christmas breakfast is still on. And you had better get into that car and drive through the snow because the sun is shining here."

I got on the line and Doris said, "You did what? Halfway to Greensboro and you didn't call me before turning back?"

We sheepishly drank a cup of hot coffee and ate some of Ralph's donuts before we got back into the car and headed for highway 421 one more time. Harold and Ralph were still praying.

Sure enough, the snow got worse, but we kept going. "Doris said the sun was shining on the other side," we kept reminding ourselves. We drove carefully—and prayed. We had never driven in snow before.

With a sigh of relief we came to Dunn, halfway to Greensboro, and stopped at the Waffle House. The Christian owners greeted us like relatives—and that's not all. The sun *was* shining! No snow! Not one flake!

We had turned back too soon!

165

Needless to say, we didn't meet Grace and Doris for lunch, Chris and Peggy had limited time to shop, and I didn't write one word.

When Saturday morning came and we all gathered at Trinity Church for the annual Christmas breakfast, the sun was still shining.

During the program I told about "our blizzard," and we all laughed together. I continued, "We asked directions from a man who told the truth about the snow getting worse down the road. It was only as far as he had gone, so he turned back. The news was quite different at the end of the line."

It is often the same in life's storms. We ask directions from those who are still in the storm. God has sent messages from the other side of it: "The sun is shining." He tells us that eyes or ears haven't begun to see the glories beyond the storm.

Moses viewed the Promised Land from a mountain. God let him see beyond the storm. John, on the Isle of Patmos, saw beyond the storm and sent directions.

Throughout the ages God's people shout the song of victory:

> *When we all get to heaven,*
> *What a day of rejoicing that will be!*

Jesus told His disciples that they were going to the other side of the lake. He didn't tell them about the storm. (See Matthew, chapter 8.)

Faith reads the present in the light of the future

and God uses the storms to strengthen our faith. The enemy of fear can't overthrow us until we overthrow ourselves.

In turning back too soon and not calling ahead for directions, we defeated ourselves. We were almost out of the path of the storm and didn't know it.

Looking over the audience, I recalled how Roy Putnam, a young pastor with a small group of Christians, converts from the early Greensboro, North Carolina Crusade, began Trinity Church.

> *The warning echoed in the wind, "Stay close to the fence!"*

For more than thirty years this brilliant man used his dynamic prayers and Bible teaching to bless thousands. The beautiful sanctuary at Trinity stands as a mighty nail of truth in a sure place.

Then God took him home.

For many years he had taught the people how to live, and through the deep waters of suffering he taught us how to die. He saw a glimpse of the Son on the other side and went home with praise to God on his lips.

My heart ached as I watched Mrs. Putnam, quiet, strong, and faithful, together with her children and the entire church family, go through their storm. But Roy Putnam's faithful teaching came back to tell them, "The sun is shining on the other side."

When my father was lost in a blizzard up in Northern Canada, he cried out, "Oh, God, I am lost, but

You are not lost. Lead me to a safe place."

A warm presence drew near and Papa was led to people in a cabin nearly submerged in snow drifts. The storm passed and Papa was able to come home on Christmas Eve.

When my husband Harold's family lived in the West (Colorado), his mother would warn the children when they went off to school, "Stay close to the fence. Don't cut across the fields where the snowdrifts are deep and treacherous." The warning echoed in the wind, *Stay close to the fence!*

We can't take the chance of cutting across the fields of man's philosophy. Jesus said, "I am the way, the truth, and the life. No man cometh unto the Father, but by me" (John 14:6).

The message still comes from the Father's house: "The sun is shining on the other side."

THE CROSSBEAM

Faith is the tree from which all graces spring.

Towering fir trees stood like giant, silent sentinels around the old New Hampshire lodge, shrouding the sky. Snow fell softly covering the trees with a mantle of glistening diamonds, leaving the lodge wrapped in the stillness of a winter wonderland. Inside the lodge, giant logs blazed and crackled in a stone fireplace, spreading the warmth of glowing timbers around the room.

The women came from their dormitories, their booted feet crunching against the snow-packed walkways. They came expectantly — yet sadly — to this final session of their 1988 women's retreat. But moments later they filled the empty, rustic lodge with the sound of music and laughter.

I stood to speak, saying, "Our theme this weekend has been from Isaiah 22:23: *I have fastened you as a nail in a sure place.* So hang in there."

I told the women to look up at the crossbeam of the lodge, and observe closely the pegs, spikes and nails that held the crossbeam in place. I said to them, "Imagine for a moment, that during the night, each nail decided to pull out. Slowly, gradually, little by little, one by one, the nails left and the strength of the beam weakened, then fell, bringing the lodge down."

I linked that grave possibility to society for about fifty years ago the nails of our society decided to begin pulling out.

The spitballs and chewing gum of fifty years ago have deteriorated into murder and rape now.

Fathers, then mothers, left the home, one by one, to find an illusionary self-fulfillment. When men and women refuse to yield to the authority and standards of the one true God, eventually each one bows to a lesser god. Proud people bow to the god of power; sensual people bow to the god of pleasure; covetous people bow to the god of money.

One day my daughter Jan asked her grandmother, "What is the secret of your happy Christian life?"

"A thankful heart," was the answer. "*In everything give thanks* must be a way of life. An unthankful heart can lead us to the abyss of any sin."

We are all lovers: lovers of pleasure, lovers of money, lovers of work—or lovers of God. Whatever is uppermost in our time or effort, that is the god that controls us.

When parents decide to serve lesser gods, the children come home but there is nothing to hold on to. Home, the crossbeam of civilization, gradually weakens, and the house comes down. The children wander into a far country searching for something to give them stability.

Something has come tumbling down when the spitballs and chewing gum of fifty years ago have deteriorated into murder and rape now, only a generation later. Yes, something must have come tumbling down, and it has: the home. Satan has huffed and puffed until he has blown the wind of doubt against the faith of America and the world.

Faith is the crossbeam of the home. Little by little, the gods of the secular age turn the attention away from the authority of God's standards. The *heart* must be the sanctuary for truth, and the *home* must remain the guardian of the standards set by God.

Spurgeon said, "Once the truth of God is driven into the human heart, no power can dislodge it. Truth is not a guest, but Master of the house."

Faith is the tree from which all graces spring; it makes the weak nails strong, the doubtful nails resolute, the timid nails courageous.

No wonder Satan huffs and puffs to blow our faith down. The *cross* is the crossbeam of our faith.

The center of our salvation is the cross of Jesus

171

Christ — the point where God and sinful man merge with a crash and the way to life is opened. Oswald Chambers says, "The crash was on the heart of God."

I told the women at the retreat that once again we had been brought out of the unholy arena of a culture, increasingly hostile to God's standards, and for a few hours we had been brought into the sanctuary of His presence.

"As we draw strength from this sanctuary," I said, "you and I must go forth to be the music in a discordant world, the river in a dry place, and the love in a world of fear and hate. Before we return to a world where the winds blow against our faith, we must kneel once more at Calvary, the pivot upon which all time turns.

"Behind our obedience is the reality of the cross, that 'old rugged cross, so despised by the world,' the crossbeam of our faith.

"Jesus could have come down, but He stayed, nailed to the cross. He was fastened, in a sure place, for you and me.

"One glorious day, Jesus will reign as King of Kings. From every tribe and nation will come all those NAILS who stayed, fastened by His grace, in a sure place."

* * *

P. S. For me, it was time to go home. Time to leave the snow on the fir trees of New Hampshire and return to the sea where the wind blows through the pampas grass—home to where the ocean rolls and the sea gulls cry. To me, the song of all nature is the same as my own:

> *Then sings my soul, my Savior God, to Thee:*
> *How great Thou art, how great Thou art!"*

* * *

THE NAIL

> *Fastened by You,*
> *This nail, broken, bruised,*
> *A vessel marred by sin,*
> *Can this be used?*
>
> *Fastened by You,*
> *This lonely, empty thing,*
> *With shattered dreams,*
> *And broken wing?*
>
> *Fastened for me?*
> *Through blinding tears I see*
> *Your nail-pierced hand,*
> *Fastened to a tree.*
>
> *Fastened by You?*
> *Amazing love, and grace;*
> *A broken nail, forgiven,*
> *Fastened in God's place.*

—Margaret T. Jensen

People Making A Difference

Family Bookshelf offers the finest in good wholesome Christian literature, written by best-selling authors. All books are recommended by an Advisory Board of distinguished writers and editors.

We are also a vital part of a compassionate outreach called **Bowery Mission Ministries**. Our evangelical mission is devoted to helping the destitute of the inner city.

Our ministries date back more than a century and began by aiding homeless men lost in alcoholism. Now we also offer hope and Gospel strength to homeless, inner-city women and children. Our goal, in fact, is to end homelessness by teaching these deprived people how to be independent with the Lord by their side.

Downtrodden, homeless men are fed and clothed and may enter a discipleship program of one-on-one professional counseling, nutrition therapy and Bible study. This same Christian care is provided at our women and children's shelter.

We also welcome nearly 1,000 underprivileged children each summer at our Mont Lawn Camp located in Pennsylvania's beautiful Poconos. Here, impoverished youngsters enjoy the serenity of nature and an opportunity to receive the teachings of Jesus Christ. We also provide year-round assistance through teen activities, tutoring in reading and writing, Bible study, family counseling, college scholarships and vocational training.

During the spring, fall and winter months, our children's camp becomes a lovely retreat for religious gatherings of up to 200. Excellent accommodations include heated cabins, chapel, country-style meals and recreational facilities. Write to Paradise Lake Retreat Center, Box 252, Bushkill, PA 18324 or call: (717) 588-6067.

Still another vital part of our ministry is **Christian Herald magazine**. Our dynamic, bimonthly publication focuses on the true personal stories of men and women who, as "doers of the Word," are making a difference in their lives and the lives of others.

Bowery Mission Ministries are supported by voluntary contributions of individuals and bequests. Contributions are tax deductible. Checks should be made payable to Bowery Mission.

 Fully accredited Member of the Evangelical Council for Financial Accountability

Every Monday morning, our ministries staff joins together in prayer. If you have a prayer request for yourself or a loved one, simply write to us.

 Administrative Office: 40 Overlook Drive, Chappaqua, New York 10514 Telephone: (914) 769-9000